Single

PETER J. STEIN

A SPECTRUM BOOK

PRENTICE-HALL, INC. Englewood Cliffs, New Jersey

Library of Congress Cataloging in Publication Data

Stein, Peter J
  Single

  (A Spectrum Book)
  Includes index.
    1. Single people—United States. I. Title.
HQ800.S77   301.44   76–12642
ISBN 0–13–810572–3
ISBN 0–13–810564–2 pbk.

© 1976 by Prentice-Hall, Inc., Englewood Cliffs, New Jersey

A Spectrum Book

10 9 8 7 6 5 4 3 2 1

Printed in the United States of America

Prentice-Hall International, Inc., *London*
Prentice-Hall of Australia Pty. Limited, *Sydney*
Prentice-Hall of Canada, Ltd., *Toronto*
Prentice-Hall of India Private Limited, *New Delhi*
Prentice-Hall of Japan, Inc., *Tokyo*
Prentice-Hall of Southeast Asia Pte. Ltd., *Singapore*

For
N.S.R.

Contents

Preface

Single is intended to provide a broad overview of some of the experiences of a group of today's single men and women—their experiences in the working world, in their relationships with friends, lovers, parents, and in the larger society around them. Singles experience various social pressures to conform to contradictory social expectations, and this book reports on how singles are dealing with these pressures.

This book is not intended to be a definitive work on unmarried adults, nor is it intended to be a comprehensive review of the findings and of the writings available. It is intended to introduce the reader to the singles' world, to begin to identify the large group of singles in America. It is hoped that it will speak to singles and marrieds alike and will help to dispel some of the harmful stereotypes to which singles are now subject. *Single* and other current studies are only the beginning. We need to know a lot more about the nation's 47 million unmarried adults.

I received the encouragement and advice of many friends throughout the project. The participants at the 1975 Groves

Conference in Dubrovnik, Yugoslavia provided important initial impetus. Joel Abel, Lynn Donovan, Natalie Hannon, and Sally Wimer were most helpful at various stages of manuscript development. Lucile Duberman and Keith Melville read the entire manuscript and provided many insightful comments. Kim Curran and Elinor Schuman provided valuable research assistance, and Judy Lilleston was skillful in conducting some of the interviews. Tim Oliver typed the manuscript with care. Benjamin Zablocki of the Urban Communes Project at Columbia University and Mat Greenwald of the Institute of Life Insurance made their unpublished data available to me. At Prentice-Hall, my special thanks go to Lynne Lumsden, my editor, who kept pushing, and to Judy Joseph for her initial encouragement. My colleagues and students at Lehman College provided a supportive environment. Finally, I am most grateful to the single men and women who gave of their time and shared their lives with me.

Chapter 1
An Overview of
Singles in America

I am a sociologist. I have been teaching undergraduate courses on marriage and the family for about eight years. In my classes, we have talked about dating, pre-marital sex, marriage, children, parents, and divorce, but we have never discussed singles. It suddenly occurred to me that I had made a serious omission. I am single myself. The course I have been teaching left me and some 47 million others completely out of the social picture.[1]

You may be a student in a sociology course on the family, on sex roles, or on interpersonal relations. You may be a city-dwelling single or a mother whose twenty-six-year-old daughter is unmarried and living alone. You may be a young professional woman whose lover has just left your apartment to return to his wife. You may be a commuter waiting for the 5:16, trying to understand the single

[1] In 1975 there were 47,104,000 single, separated, divorced, and widowed men and women over the age of 18 in the United States. See Table X in the Appendix for details.

1

colleagues who share your office and lunch hours, but who lead a very different life from yours after hours. This book speaks to single and married people about the experience of being single in America and explains why more and more men and women are choosing to be single. Until now, little has been done to look at the lives of the forty-seven million men and women over the age of eighteen who are not married.

Hopefully this book will answer some of your questions about what it means to be unmarried in America.

THE STEREOTYPED SINGLE

There is a lot of mystification about single people. Married people have distorted views about the lives of singles; singles themselves have distorted views about the lives of other singles, except those of close friends. Singles are stereotyped, as are all groups; and stereotyping perpetuates the confusion about who singles are and what their lives are really like. When asked to free-associate with the word "single," singles themselves most often first said: "sex," "happiness," "loneliness," "fun," "alone,"—or, "married."

The responses and associations reflects the broad range of meanings the word "single" has in our culture. For most Americans, to be single means to belong to one of two stereotyped groups. Singles are *swingers*—the beautiful people who are constantly going to parties, who have uncommitted lives—and a lot of uncommitted sex. The men resemble Robert Redford, Joe Namath, or Billy Dee Williams. The women all look like Julie Christie, Lola Felana, or Diane Keaton. They frolic on clean, sun-drenched beaches and ski the French Alps. They drink Pepsi-Cola. They shop at Lord and Taylor or Nieman Marcus. They vacation in the Hamptons or Rehobeth Beach or with the Club Méditerranée. During the winter, they go to the Caribbean or to Mexico. They have clear complexions and blonde hair, and they look like self-assured winners. They are never ill, never poor, and *never* overweight.

Or, singles are the stereotypical Sheila Levines of the world, the *lonely losers*. They are dramatically depressed a great deal of the time, even to the point of being on the verge of suicide. They see a Park Avenue therapist twice a week. They live by themselves and consume great quantities of frozen TV dinners and diet sodas. The women in the group are in constant communication with their mothers, who periodically send them clippings from the local paper announcing yet another engagement of a former high school class-mate. The men in this group visit their mothers every other Sunday. They live by themselves and drink a lot.

Single men and women are either "with it" or "out of it." While such stereotypes may be useful to sell products, to show on tele-vision commercials, and as subject matter for novels and movies, they neither help us to understand the lives of singles, nor do they help singles themselves to deal realistically with their lives.

An examination of the lives of single men and women suggests that neither stereotype is accurate. Single people reveal a number of different experiences. Their lives are filled with exciting experi-ences and lonely times, with personal growth and with moments of depression, with feelings of belonging and of isolation, with both a clear sense of who they are and with times of confusion. Yet, overall, single men and women report many more positive experiences than negative ones.

Serious research about singles is notably missing from the field of family sociology. There are a few valuable studies of those previously married, such as Helena Lopata's study of widowhood (1973), William Goode's study of divorced women (1956), Jessie Bernard's study of second marriage (1956), Lucile Duberman's study of reconstituted families (1975) and Roxanne Hiltz's study of social services needed by the widowed (forthcoming). Margaret Adams' "The Single Woman in Today's Society" (1974) and her forthcoming book, *Single Blessedness* (1976), offer positive inter-pretations of the single life. Robert Staples is studying single black men and women (in preparation). An examination of leading texts in family sociology revealed that only a few deal with singles, and, even then, rather briefly. When not completely ignored by most of the writers on the family, singles are defined in terms of their relationship to marriage. Duberman (1974) faces the issue squarely:

> Sociologists are as human and as culture-bound as anyone else and thus tend to ignore those elements of society that do not conform to our cultural norms. This obvious omission [of texts on singles] tells us something about our society and our discipline. Surely the oversight is not because sociologists are unaware that a sizeable proportion of our population is unmarried. Rather, the neglect reflects our adherence to the ideal that everyone should marry and that, if he really wants to, anyone can.

In our society, adulthood and emotional maturity are held to be synonymous with marriage and parenthood. The good life is defined as the married life. Any choice of a life style that leads a marriage-able person away from the social obligation to pair off and settle down is considered wrong. The person who chooses singlehood is seen as immature at best, or even self-destructive. The attitude prevails that those who remain single are deviant or in some way inadequate for adult roles.

Social psychologists are accustomed to referring to singles as "those who fail to marry," or as "those who do not make positive choices." In psychological and sociological literature, if singlehood is discussed at all, it is generally in terms of singles as being hostile toward marriage or toward persons of the opposite sex, as being homosexual; as fixating on parents; as unattractive, or as having physical or financial obstacles to finding a mate; as unwilling to assume responsibility, or afraid of involvement; as unable to do well in the dating/mating game or having unrealistic criteria for finding a mate; as perceiving marriage as a threat to a career or as being in geographical, educational, or occupational isolation. The possibility that some people might actually choose to be single because they want to be, because they feel it would contribute to their growth and well-being to remain so, is simply not believed possible.

Considering the strong negative value placed on singlehood, it is somewhat surprising that more research has not been done on the subject, if only in the interests of explaining it away. Instead, the eye of research remains averted from the phenomenon of singles and riveted on the family.

Why?

THE AMERICAN FAMILY PATTERN

People are conditioned to accept marriage and the family as the natural arrangement: A girl becomes a woman through marriage and motherhood; a boy becomes a man through his role as father and provider. How else could it be? Hasn't it always been this way?

In fact, the family has been around for a long time. Some form of the family has been identified in all known societies, although the nuclear family based on the romantic couple is a relatively recent Western development. Whether it is extended, polygamous, or nuclear, the family does serve certain basic functions. The first of these is the *reproductive,* or the replacement function. Second, there is *status placement,* or the means by which the individual's identity and chances within his or her society are determined. This is the integrative or maintenance function. Third, there is the *socialization,* or the child-rearing function, wherein offspring learn socially appropriate attitudes and behavior and socially approved sex roles. In this way the family operates as the instrument of social control by imparting social values and culture.

There are other tasks performed by the family in the service of maintaining the larger society. Prior to industrialization, the family performed the major economic, protective, religious, recreational, and educational functions. With modernization, it has been said that the family has come to lose many of these functions. Yet in this precarious condition, the nuclear family today retains three major functions: consumption, socialization, and emotional support.

It is important to ask how well the family performs these functions and for whom? There is a crucial difference between identifying a social need and fulfilling that need. Whose needs are being met and whose needs are being violated?

There is little dispute about the family's consuming functions—the economy persuades the family to purchase the goods produced by industry. The economic system requires a high degree of purchasing and "there is powerful economic impetus for people to marry, create homes, and have children, so that they will purchase those things that are necessary for the maintenance of society" (Duberman, 1974:21).

The second function, socialization, is the process through which the newlyborn becomes human. It is only through interaction with other people that we become members of a social group. We are what our experience has been with the people who are important to us. The first social group we experience is the family.

The child's early years within the family are crucial, since it is there that he or she learns what to value and what to reject, what is to be regarded as important and what is unimportant, what to strive for, and when it is not disastrous to fail. The little boy who gets father's approval and attention every time he plays well in a ball game strives to become a good ballplayer. When mother praises her young daughter's drawings, she tries to become a better artist. On the other hand, where there is lack of support for interests and activities from people who care, there is little likelihood of development.

Parents and children relate to each other in the social setting of the family. Parents have already been socialized, and they are prepared and predisposed to inculcate the values, beliefs, and life styles they have assimilated. Our sense of who we are, then, emerges out of contact, communication, and control by others. It is within the structure of the family that the process of personality development and socialization are most likely to occur. It is the family that maintains and creates a common culture for its members.

Many family sociologists have argued that perhaps the most important function performed by the family is that of emotional support. In a fragmented world, the family institution is supposed to offer solace, succor, support, and sex. However, the increasing divorce rate indicates that the family does not always provide emotional support. It is also possible for people to obtain emotional support outside of marriage. There are multiple options resulting from the greater sexual liberation, from the women's movement, and the general trend towards more open relationships. Yet most people have been socialized, from an early age, into believing that we can only meet our emotional needs in the family.

GROWING UP TO GET MARRIED

In a study of fifth and sixth graders in the United States (eleven and twelve year olds), Carlfred Broderick and George Rowe (1968), found that eighty-four per cent of girls and sixty-two per cent of boys expected eventual marriage and that seventy-four per cent already had boyfriends or girlfriends. Of those who had such friends, sixty-six per cent reported that they were or had been in love.

Dating, the practice which is supposed to get boys and girls ready for marriage, starts early. Statistically, dating is successful: Most Americans marry, and about twenty-five per cent more than once. But dating, which is based on traditional sex roles, includes much stereotyping and heavy doses of anxiety, competitiveness, and jealousy. Willard Waller (1937) speaks of the "rating/dating" complex, wherein men and women meet and rate each other in terms of marketable characteristics such as good looks, wealth, prestige, possessions, type of car, and the amount of money spent by the man on the woman to "show her a good time." People relate to each other as objects possessing certain marketable and quantifiable characteristics. The system can then exploit those who have scarce resources.

While some argue that things have changed since Waller's analysis, Mirra Komarovsky (1973) found that college men were still bound by sex stereotypes and played traditional male roles when on dates with women. Thus, the power of sex role stereotypes persists. The idea of finding Mr. or Ms. Right is also supported by movies, the mass media, television, and pop culture. It may no longer be Nelson Eddy and Jeaneatte McDonald, but Robert Redford and Diane Keaton are still falling in love the way Eddy and McDonald did. We are taught to seek the romantic ideal—one person to fulfill all of our needs in an intense, meaningful relationship.

THE SINGLES BUSINESS

The stereotypes and the traditional rating/dating game is further supported by the "singles industry," which, in the United States, is a $40 billion-a-year industry consisting of singles' bars, singles' resorts, and singles' housing complexes (Jacoby, 1974). In 1973, Chateau D'Vie opened up in New York State, selling memberships to a year-round singles' country club at $600 per person. In a few months, they sold over one thousand memberships. Several other singles-only resorts have opened since then.

But such commercial enterprises do not provide real alternatives to marriage. Indeed, they are geared to getting singles married and, as such, they meet the needs of entrepreneurs and business people much more than they meet the needs of singles. They are simply updated versions of the rating/dating complex in a more sophisticated and expensive setting than that of high school or college.

Parents and relatives constantly exert pressure toward marriage. They want their children to have a marriage like they had, except perhaps a little better. This is poignantly illustrated in Gail Parent's 1973 novel, *Sheila Levine is Dead and Living in New York*. The heroine is greeted at her sister's wedding with best wishes for hers. She tries to commit suicide, an attempt that is as unsuccessful as is her hunt for a husband.

So the family and society unite through socialization to make most of us feel that marriage is a natural arrangement. Those who do not think so are regarded as odd, strange, or deviant. There is an inevitability to this process. The cultural imperative dictates marriage and the family; an imperative that reaches its greatest impact when we come to think of marriage as the most natural and taken-for-granted process. The effectiveness of such an imperative leaves no choice to see or do otherwise. As Duberman states: "Ours is a two-by-two world, and there is little room in it for the unaccompanied individual . . . To justify their own state, married people think of marriage as 'natural,' and anyone who does not conform to this point of view is challenging the social values" (Duberman, 1974:115).

To be single has been seen in relation to marriage and the family. Without "the family," the concept of "single" has had no meaning. Single is a word used to categorize a vast and divergent group of persons in order to treat them on the basis of one common criterion—their non-marriage. Marriage is seen as a positive choice, a positive category. Single implies the opposite: a negative choice, a bad state. The available words reflect the culturally desirable state. Single implies less desirable, lacking a partner, not complete, alone. We lack the word to describe *persons* who lead lives, hold jobs, have fun, experience hard times; in short, who do all things persons do, but who prefer *not* to be married? We lump together, in one category, a very divergent group of persons. It is the purpose of this book to begin to find out who these people really are.

Chapter 2
Who Are the Singles?

The term "singles" presents several problems. Besides the fact that it's a meaningless label, except in reference to another group (the marrieds), it's a label that is attached to some very different types of people. Are singles everyone who's unmarried? Or should "single" include only those who have never married? Should the term "single" include those persons living together but not married? What are the differences between the divorced, the separated, and the widowed; between those who choose to be single and those who don't; between those who are of college age and those who are older? In this chapter we examine the experiences of some of these types of singles.

Yet all these people, with their different experiences, needs, and life styles are lumped into the one vast, homogeneous group that is collectively called "single." Because of the way it is currently being used, "single" is an inaccurate and misleading term. So, for the purposes of this book, our working definition of "single" will be: those men and women who are not currently married or involved in an exclusive heterosexual or homosexual relationship.

We exclude cohabiting singles from the term because the inter-personal experiences of cohabiting couples tend to parallel the interpersonal experiences of marrieds. A "marriage-like" experi-ence is the way most men and women describe their cohabitation.

Researchers questioning college students living together have indicated that students consider their relationship to be a trial marriage, companionate marriage, or two-stage marriage. Eleanor Macklin (1972) has suggested that living together may be a "natural component of a strong, affectionate 'dating' relationship, a living out of 'going steady'—which may grow into something more but which, in the meantime is . . . pleasurable in and of itself." Whether or not it "grows into something else" is generally a function of the relationship and the ages of the partners. For some, living together includes being open to other dating relationships yet, for a majority, cohabiting appears to parallel the monogamous marriage experience.

TRENDS

The late 1930s were characterized by low birth rates and delayed marriages. The nation was just coming out of an economic depres-sion, fewer people were getting married, and fewer couples were having children. The average age at first marriage was rising, and almost ten per cent of women over fifty years old had never married. Almost twenty per cent of American women bore no children during their lifetimes, and many of the children expected by population experts never arrived. During World War II, marriage and birth rates remained low while millions of women, married and single, entered the labor force.

After World War II, the picture changed dramatically.[1] Marriage and divorce rates increased rapidly at first, then fell sharply. By the mid-1950s, couples were entering marriage at the youngest ages on record; all but four per cent of those at the height of the child-bearing period were married. The baby boom that began with the return of servicemen reached a peak in the mid-1950s, and did not

[1] This section draws on Paul Glick's study: "Some Recent Changes in American Families," *Current Population Reports,* P-23, No. 52 (1975).

diminish significantly until after 1960. Demographers were predicting that, of the young people of the 1960s, all but three to four per cent would eventually marry.

But by the late 1960s, fewer Americans were opting for the family life style of the 1950s. The marriage rate among single persons under forty-five years of age was again as low as it had been at the end of the Depression.

Over the past several years, it has been evident from census data that there has been an increase in the singles population and a decrease in the married population. (See Table I comparing 1970 and 1975 census data.)

Table I

Trends in Marital Status 1970-1975[a]

Year	Married	Divorced	Separated	Single	Widowed
			MEN		
1975	62.3	3.3	1.6	29.5	2.4
1974	63.1	3.1	1.5	29.0	2.5
1970	64.3	2.2	1.3	28.1	2.9
Percentage of Change 1970 to 1975:	—3.1	+ 50.0	+ 23.0	+ 4.9	—17.2
			WOMEN		
1975	56.9	4.8	2.8	22.8	12.1
1974	57.5	4.4	2.7	22.5	11.9
1970	58.4	3.5	2.2	22.1	12.5
Percentage of Change 1970 to 1975:	—2.6	+ 37.1	+ 27.2	+ 3.1	—3.2

[a]Percentage of total U.S. population 14 years of age and over.

Source: Jessie Bernard, "Note on Changing Life Styles, 1970-1974," *Journal of Marriage and the Family* 37 (1975), p. 583. Also U.S. Bureau of the Census, *Current Population Reports,* P-20, no. 287, "Marital Status and Living Arrangements: March 1975." (Washington, D.C.: U.S. Government Printing Office, 1975), Table 1.

In comparing 1970 and 1974 data, Jessie Bernard (1975) indicated that the "direction rather than the magnitude of discernible change is most interesting." Although the most dramatic rise over the four years is in the proportion of men and women who were separated or divorced, there was also a marked increase in the never-married category. At the same time, there was a decrease in the proportion of men and women who were married and living with their spouses. An increase in mean age at first marriage reflects an increase in marriage postponement for men and women.

The trends identified by Bernard in 1974 continued into 1975. What she termed the "spectacular rate of increase in the proportions of both men and women who were separated or divorced" between 1970 and 1974 has continued its acceleration into 1975. From 1970 to 1975, the proportion divorced increased—thirty seven percent for women and fifty percent for men—a dramatic percentage increase even though we are dealing with a still small proportion of the overall population.

In 1960, the median age at first marriage for women was 20.3; in 1975 it increased to 21.1. The corresponding median age for men at first marriage was 22.8 in 1960, and 23.5 in 1975.[2]

THE YOUNG NEVER-MARRIED SINGLES

The fifteen-year period from 1960 to 1975 has seen an increase in the percentage of both men and women between the ages of twenty and twenty nine who have remained single.[3] Table II documents this increase.

Why have more and more young adults decided to postpone marriage? Paul Glick suggests that part of the answer lies in the fact that nearly three times as many women were enrolled in college in 1972 as in 1960, an increase from 1.2 million to 3.5 million. Glick

[2]U.S. Bureau of the Census, *Current Population Reports,* P-20, No. 287, "Marital Status and Living Arrangements: March 1975" (Washington, D.C.: U.S. Government Printing Office, 1975), pp. 2-3.

[3]Much of the data cited in this section appear in summary form in Table X of the Appendix: "Marital Status of the Population (age 18 and over), by Sex and Age, 1975."

also identifies the "marriage squeeze"—an excess of young women at the currently "most marriageable" age. Women born during the baby boom after World War II reached the average marriage age two or three years before men born at the same time reached their average marriage age.

Table II
Change in Men and Women
Remaining Single (1960-1975)

	1960	1975
Women Remaining Single:		
Age 20-24	28.4%	40.3%
Age 25-29	10.5%	13.8%
Men Remaining Single:		
Age 20-24	53.1%	59.9%
Age 25-29	20.8%	22.3%

Source: U.S. Bureau of the Census, *Current Population Reports,* Marital Status and Living Arrangements: March 1975, U.S. Government Printing Office, Washington, D.C., 1975, p. 2.

Other factors, such as the women's movement, the expanding economic and employment opportunities for women, and the increasing availability of birth-control methods, have probably contributed to marriage postponement as well.

According to Glick (1975:4):

> . . . it is too early to predict with confidence that the increase in singleness among the young will lead to an eventual decline in life-time marriage [but], just as cohorts of young women who have postponed childbearing for an unusually long time seldom make up for the child deficit as they grow older, so also young people who are delaying marriage may never make up for the marriage deficit later on. They may try alternatives to marriage and they may like them.

Glick notes the movement away from marriage and family norms, particularly when it comes into conflict with the full potential of individuals. The emergence of singlehood as a freely chosen life style can be conducive to meeting people's needs for growth and supportive interpersonal relationships.

Supporting evidence for the decreasing attraction of marriage and the corresponding increase of young singles comes from attitudinal studies. In a 1962 study of unmarried college women, Robert Bell found that "only two per cent of them had little or no interest in future marriage." (1971:157) A decade later, unmarried college women were queried in their freshman and senior years. There were significant shifts in attitudes toward marriage. In 1969, as first year students, only three per cent of the sample did not expect to marry. As seniors in 1973, eight per cent did not expect to marry—and a startling forty per cent of the women said they did not know whether or not they would marry (Stein, 1973).

The same study showed that thirty per cent of senior men and women felt that traditional marriage is becoming obsolete; twenty-five per cent agreed with the statement that the traditional family structure of mother, father, and children living under one roof no longer works. This parallels national trends in student values as cited in the Daniel Yankelovitch survey of *The Changing Values On Campus* (1972), which reports that the number of students who believe that the present institution of marriage is becoming obsolete has increased from twenty-four per cent in 1969, to twenty-eight per cent in 1970, thirty-four percent in 1971. In 1971, in response to questions about marriage and the family structure (questions that were not asked in earlier years), thirty-two per cent of the students did not look forward to being married or were not sure about it, and twenty-nine per cent either disagreed that the traditional family structure works or were not sure about it.

How are these young people, who tend toward negative views and expectations of marriage, confronting a society that seems to offer so few alternatives outside of marriage?

As indicated by the census figures, they tend to be postponing marriage. Their major goals upon graduating from high school or college seem to be toward jobs that offer reasonable incomes and allow for growth and a display of competence (Starr & Carns, 1972). They also seek enjoyable life styles. As a group, they have a growing discretionary income, which indicates a step beyond minimal economic independence from their parents.

For some, an important task is in developing new friends in new settings; they move from the campus to cities, seeking the opportunity to form relationships with peers who may hold values and have behavior patterns that are significantly different from those of their families. There they cope with the fears of living in a vast, anonymous, often alienating environment. There they also rub elbows with a variety of people and get a chance to turn some fantasies into real life. The stereotype of the young single depicted in magazines like *Playboy* or *Cosmopolitan* may romanticize the dazzle; but young singles in the cities do have opportunities for learning, for gaining valuable life experience—and for having fun.

Their young married counterparts may experience similar situations, but with one major exception. For the most part, they become more and more reliant on *one* other person to provide much of the support and encouragement they need.

Findings from a national sample of married and single men and women presented in Table III reveal some of the differences between the two groups. For each of the responses below, the differences between men and women were smaller than the differences between those who were married and those who were single.

Table III
Attitudinal Differences Between Never-Married and Married Adults

Most Important Life Goal	*Married*	*Never-Married*
A happy family life.	87%	50%
The opportunity to develop as an individual.	9%	35%
A fulfilling career.	1%	11%
Importance of forming and preserving the traditional family.	83%	67%

Source: Institute of Life Insurance, *Current Social Issues,* 1975.

With respect to attitudes toward various movements for social change, the never-married are more liberal in their responses than are the marrieds. They are more supportive of women's liberation, birth control, communal living, civil rights, legalized marijuana, and anti-war movements than are married persons. In all of these issues, the attitudes of the separated and divorced are quite similar to the attitudes of the never-marrieds, whereas the attitudes of the widowed are quite similar to the attitudes of married persons.

THE OLDER NEVER-MARRIED SINGLES

Glick (1975) focused on a group of women born during the Depression years of the 1930s who are currently between thirty-five and forty-four years old. Their generation experienced the earliest average age for first marriage on record, a high birth rate, and one of the lowest proportions of singles on record. (Only five per cent had never been married.) Of the group, women with higher levels of education were more likely to remain single than their less-educated sisters. About eight per cent of women college graduates with no graduate school training remained single by 1970. And about twenty per cent with graduate school training remained single by 1970. In 1970, one in every five women around the age of forty with some graduate school education, or with an income of $20,000 or more, has not married—compared to only one in every twenty women with no college education (Glick, 1975:5).

Women with higher levels of education and professional training clearly have more options for interesting careers; they also have more opportunities, including combining a career with being a wife and a mother.

Bernard (1972) reports that women who remain single are superior to single men in terms of education, occupation, and income.

At every age level, the average single woman surpasses the average single male. They are often upwardly mobile. (1972:34) Moreover, they, more than married women, pulled themselves up educationally and professionally. They reflect a strong achievement orientation and a desire to succeed. (1972:38) At ages 45 to 54, the gap [between single men and women] is a veritable chasm. The single women are more educated, have higher average incomes and are in higher occupations. (1972:34)

Glick suggests that, at the same time, these women may find it harder to find men who will not feel threatened by a woman's career success, or by the likelihood of an egalitarian marriage.

The life style and experience of the older singles group differ from those of the young singles. The older singles are less preoccupied with learning how to get along in the world and more concerned with career expansion. They have money to spend on leisure activities or advanced educational pursuits (Glick, 1975:6).

While life can be active and stimulating for older singles, it is also possible that they can be more vulnerable to despair and resignation than younger singles. The secretly wished-for mate has not been found, and the prospect of lonely later years can be frightening. If an older single has not established a broad base of supportive and tender relationships, the middle years can be a period of depression and deterioration.

A number of studies have reported that older unmarried men, especially, are likely to show mental health problems, including depression, severe neurotic symptoms, phobic tendencies and passivity. They also report being less happy than married men and they are more likely to commit suicide than married men. In a study of mental health in Manhattan, Leo Srole (1972) found that about twice as many never-married men as never-married women showed mental health impairments. Several national studies report that single women "experience less discomfort than single men; are more active . . . work through the problems they face and appear in most ways stronger in meeting the challenges of their positions than men" (Gurin, Veroff and Feld, cited in Bernard 1972:33).

How can this be explained?

More than seventy-five years ago, Emile Durkheim, (1897) a noted French sociologist, developed the crucial sociological idea that social integration and social disorganization have important effects on individual behavior. His study of suicide and the variation in suicide rates among different groups revealed that the greater the social bonds surrounding and supporting the individual, the smaller the chance of suicide; and, conversely, the fewer the bonds, the greater the likelihood that the individual will try to destroy himself. Differences in suicide rates among the major religious groups supported Durkheim's thesis. The more closely-knit religious communities had lower suicide rates than the more loosely structured religions.

If we apply Durkheim's proposition to single adults in America, we find important differences in the extent to which single men and women are integrated into support networks. There are a number of studies that suggest important differences between men and women regarding intimacy, sociability, affiliative styles, degrees of self-disclosure, and empathy. Elizabeth Douvan and Joseph Adelson (1966) found that, among adolescents, male–male friendships were less intimate than female–female friendships. Nicholas Babchuck and Alan Booth (1969) reported that participation in voluntary associations was more variable and less stable among men than among women. Alan Booth (1972) notes, in a study of adults in two urban communities, that, while males have more friends than females, male friendships tend to be less close and spontaneous than female friendships, which are affectively richer. Men exceeded women in the number of voluntary association memberships, but not in the commitment of time to group activities. Bert Adams (1968) reports that, on the average, there is less intimacy between men than between women friends. Genevieve Knupfer and associates (1966) write that, in their sample, older single males had fewer "meaningful relationships" than older single females; that single men were more isolated, had fewer friends and fewer interpersonal experiences. Seventy per cent of the men, compared to fifty-three per cent of the women, lived alone. Sixty-four per cent of the single men kept problems to themselves, compared to fifty-one per cent of the women.

Since mental illness can be related to the lack of support and care networks and, since the evidence suggests that single men are less likely to be a part of such networks, older single men will continue to show higher rates of mental illness. However, some evidence from studies cited by Pleck and Sawyer (1974), and the Zablocki study of communes (1975), suggest some changes in the direction of greater participation by older single men in friendship networks and organizations. The forthcoming Midtown Manhattan Mental Health Restudy (Srole et al., forthcoming) will update existing data on the mental health of single adult men and women.

THE DIVORCED SINGLES

Among older singles, a greater proportion are among the widowed, separated or divorced than among the never married. The divorce rate has climbed to the high level it reached soon after the end of World War II. Glick and Norton (1973) have estimated that one out of three marriages of women thirty years old had been, or would eventually be, dissolved by divorce.

Between September 1973 and August 1974, it was estimated that about 2,233,000 marriages and about 948,000 divorces took place.

For the first time since soon after World War Two, the marriage total for a 12-month period was significantly smaller (by 68,000) than it had been in the preceding year. However, the divorce total for the 12 months ending in August, 1974 had continued to rise (by 56,000) above the level for the preceding 12 months. (Glick 1975:2)

The 1.3 million persons under thirty-four years of age who are divorced but who have not remarried is more than double the 1960 figure. Thus, the growing divorce rate has also increased the number of singles, who are tending to stay unmarried for a longer period of time than did their counterparts a decade earlier.

There is a continuing trend toward a down-turn in marriage and an up-turn in divorce. The annual number of first marriages has not kept pace with the increased pool of those potentially eligible to marry. About three of four current marriages are first marriages, so the total number of marriages each year is being substantially affected by high remarriage rates among the increased number of divorced persons. Since, according to Glick (1975), some four out of five divorced persons will eventually remarry, it appears that there is an even greater trend away from *first* marriages than the down-trend in total marriage figures indicates.

Men are more likely to remarry than women. In 1970, in the thirty-five to forty-four-year-old group, 3.6 per cent of the divorced

men and 5.5 per cent of the divorced women were not remarried.
About five-sixths of the men and three-fourths of the women eventually remarry. The pool of eligibles is more limited for women
than for men, and divorced women tend to outlive divorced men.
As with the 3.6 per cent of the men who do not remarry, we
must assume that a percentage of the women also choose not to
remarry.

THE SINGLE PARENT

An important and recent trend in single life styles is in the sharp
increase of one-parent families, which currently number some 3.5
million. More than eight million children under the age of eighteen
live with their mothers; over 800,000 live with their fathers. About
one in every four children, nationwide, is being raised by a single
parent (Brandwein et al; 1974).

Even though about two-thirds of two-parent families have only
one breadwinner, (Cogswell and Sussman, 1972) the median income in two-parent families is two to three times that of one-parent
families (Brandwein et al; 1974). Because single parents often rely
on their own resources to provide support for their children, they
are in great need not only of daycare, but of twenty-four-hour child
care services, staffed by skilled adults. There is also a need for
part-time jobs that carry full benefits; for accessible recreational
and leisure activity centers; for neighborhood dental, medical, and
health care clinics that are open before and after working hours and
on weekends (Le Masters, 1974:139-156).

The economic hardships single parents and their children face
reflect the lower wages paid to all women, particularly to minority
women, who comprise a disproportionately large part of all single
mothers.

The commune is offering an alternative life style to a small
proportion of single parents, in providing economically viable and
emotionally supportive settings with peer group relationships for
both children and parents. If the conventional patterns have not
worked for them, perhaps the cooperative efforts of communal
living will (Brandwein et al; 1974).

THE SINGLES SAMPLE

The data in this book were gathered from two unrelated samples of single men and women. Sample A (also referred to as the Younger Sample) is a group of single students at a metropolitan college in the Northeast region, part of a larger sample of single and married students enrolled in the day and evening division of the college. The evening session students tend to be older than their day session counterparts, and most of them hold full-time jobs. The sample is described in Table XI of the Appendix.

The students were asked to complete a questionnaire dealing with their experiences as singles: dating, marital plans, friendships, sexual mores, occupational and educational goals.

In addition, in order to identify the major aspects of the life styles of single persons, we conducted forty in-depth interviews with twenty men and twenty women not included in Sample A. The people interviewed in Sample B (also referred to as the Older Sample) lived in the Brooklyn Heights area of New York City and in Boston, Massachusetts (The sample is described in Table XII of the Appendix). In order to sample men and women who were committed, at least for the time being, to staying single, we only included those who responded negatively to the following questions: (1) Is there one person of the opposite or same sex that you now see exclusively? (2) Do you plan to marry in the near future? (3) Do you plan to live with one person in an exclusive relationship in the near future?

A majority of the respondents were professionals. Twelve of the men were in law, teaching (high school and college), medicine, health service administration and engineering. Fourteen of the women were professionals: teachers (grade school, high school, and college), social workers, a biologist, an architect, and a clinical psychologist. The rest of the men and women were in the arts or the service occupations.

The respondents included persons who at some time in their lives had been involved in exclusive relationships, and who were thus able to assess their preferences for being single on the basis of comparative experience. They are men and women who have chosen, at least for the foreseeable future, to remain single. The quotes which appear in the text are taken from these interviews.

While making no claims for the representativeness of the sample, the long interviews revealed complex information about the single and married experience. (The interviewing schedule used is in the Appendix.)

The questionnaire completed by the Younger Sample helped to identify areas that needed probing, and the interviews with the Older Sample allowed us to chart the dynamics of the single experience: the decision to stay single, work experiences, early socialization, and the like. The author is aware of the limitations of the sample. We have not interviewed singles who are in manual, skilled, and semi-skilled occupations. Most of our respondents completed college. Only five of the forty men and women interviewed as part of the Older Sample were nonwhite. However the people in our sample all shared a common value: they viewed being single as a status that exists apart from and independent of marriage.

A comprehensive study of single adults in America awaits the well-funded researcher. Our focus is the dynamics of the single experience and the interpersonal relationships of singles.

Chapter 3
The Single and Society

There are social forces at work on single men and women: forces that affect their jobs, their living conditions, and their interpersonal relationships with peers and with their families.

On their jobs, single people may be affected by discrimination. Outright discrimination tends to show up only in certain industries, although hard data on the pervasiveness of discrimination are difficult to come by. To our knowledge, there have been no systematic studies on discrimination against singles, since the single/married category is not often included in the available statistics. However, some data do exist, and our interviewees revealed some of the patterns of discrimination.

Although the ideal may dictate that no discrimination exists on the basis of sex, race, religion, or national origin, and although that ideal may even be institutionalized by laws and statutes, the actual practice is quite different. For instance, women continue to make twenty to forty per cent less than men with the same qualifications and in the same jobs. (Ehrlich et al, 1975). So, in order to understand how society functions, we must focus on actuality rather than on ideal formulation.

JOB EXPERIENCES

According to a national survey cited in Chapter 2 (see Table III) work and careers are as central—or more central—to the lives of single adults as they are to married adults, yet in many cases, married—or even divorced—men and women are given preference over single persons with the same qualifications who have the same experience level. In a survey of fifty major corporations, it was found that eighty per cent of the responding companies asserted that marriage was not essential to upward mobility. However, a majority also indicated that only two per cent of their executives, including junior management, were single. Over sixty per cent reported that single executives tend to "make snap judgements," and twenty-five per cent believed singles to be "less stable" than married people (Jacoby, 1974).

With respect to employment, companies tend to follow the dictum that married men make a better investment in terms of responsibility, dependability, and staying power. Employers can indicate to employment agencies that they prefer married applicants over single ones, and there are no laws to prevent them from doing so.

We asked 165 men and women whether or not they had experienced discrimination because they were single. Thirty per cent of the Younger Sample and forty per cent of the Older Sample felt that they had experienced discrimination in one or several areas: in work, in obtaining credit or loans, in housing, insurance and taxation.

Larry, of the Older Sample, reported that, after succeeding in being selected for an important job over a number of other applicants, he was told that one factor working in his favor was that he had been married and was a father, supporting his son. He was told by the personnel director that his closest competitor was a single man whose qualifications were also outstanding, but who generated greater doubt in the mind of the personnel director because he had never been married. Larry was told that it was better to have been married and divorced than never to have been married at all. There must be more than the poet intended in the phrase: "'tis better to have loved and lost than never to have loved at all."

Are single persons less likely to be promoted? At the time of her interview, Ellen worked as an editor of a major publishing firm in New York and had twice been passed over for promotion. After considerable probing, she discovered that it was because she was single. Although her editorial work was judged to be outstanding, and although she had been with the company for over seven years, management feared losing her to a husband. The management assumed that an attractive and intelligent woman like Ellen would soon find a man and leave the company with her husband for parts unknown. Ellen was amused because all the men she was dating had New York jobs and would be unlikely to move. She thought that the same considerations would not be applied to a single male editor, since it would be assumed that marriage would make him more responsible and tie him down more. Yet, despite her seven years of loyalty to the company, management appeared to be convinced that she would give up her career immediately upon marriage.

Kim reported that she had worked for another major publishing house where she and several other single women discovered, through an informal contact in the personnel office, that they were being underpaid relative to their married counterparts. After appealing to management several times and being turned down on each occasion, the women began to plan collective strategy. When word of their strategy leaked out to management, several of the most active women were fired.

In the cases of both Kim and Ellen, it is difficult to separate discrimination due to sexism from discrimination due to being single. In these and other cases of salary and promotion discrimination, sexism and being single go together. For example, Natalie, a programmer, works in a predominantly male occupation. She

reported a "depressing and infuriating" conversation she had with
several of her male colleagues, all of whom were married.

> My boss couldn't, or didn't want to understand why I wasn't married.
> He imagined all sorts of orgies going on. In the other extreme, two of
> the younger guys said they felt sorry for me, that I was missing out on
> a lot of fun when I told them I was happy and that I wanted neither to
> marry nor be a mother. They looked upset. They couldn't understand
> my position, and I think they didn't believe me. I was pretty upset by it.

On further reflection, Natalie began to feel that her own cer-
tainty about remaining single had been threatening to her colleagues.
Instead of dealing with and accepting her values, they challenged
her perception of her needs and tried to convince her that she was
wrong.

Among our respondents, discrimination ranged from overt cases
to more subtle, more complex, though no less onerous cases
involving the important informal networks which exist in every
institution: business-related friendships, luncheon conversations,
and informal contacts that enter into job retention and promotion
considerations.

Anyone who has worked for an organization of any size under-
stands the importance of informal networks. Sociologists have
learned that informal networks are an important part of any
institution. In fact, informal networks may be a better index of the
operating values and norms of an organization than formal
arrangements.

Phil, an assistant professor at a major university at the time of
the interview, reflected on a subtle kind of informal network discrimination:

> It was hard being the only single person in the department. I would
> be invited to social gatherings and would get pretty nervous about who
> my date should be. The men would get into shop talk, and the women,
> in some other part of the house, would talk about their families, the
> local schools, and summer vacations. My date and I would usually feel
> uneasy—not quite fitting in and feeling a bit guilty about not fitting
> in.

Phil's experience is a reflection of the way marital status can intrude into friendship networks which, in turn, can affect formal job considerations. Clearly, other distinctions not germane for job performance may also intervene, such as race, sex, ethnic origin, or religion. Suffice it to say that, to the extent that married people have decision-making power over job hiring and promotion; to the extent that informal friendship networks affect these decisions, and to the extent that marital status influences membership in friendship networks, singles will experience discrimination.

Despite evidence of discrimination, work occupies an important place in the lives of single people. In describing the experiences of single women, Margaret Adams (1974) suggests that an indispensable factor in making single living a pleasure is the ability to be economically independent and self-supporting.

The fact that work is central to the lives of single men and women was also reported by Joyce Starr and Donald Carns in their study (1972) of young single college graduates living in Chicago. They reported that ". . . the adjustment these graduates make to the world of work, and their patterns of forming and dissolving friendships" at work and outside of work provides "their significant connections and sense of self in the urban milieu."

Most of our respondents found work to be a very important part of their lives. More than sixty per cent felt that they received some emotional support from their coworkers. Many said that they devoted longer hours to work than some of their married colleagues; that they worked at least as hard as their colleagues.

Nancy, an editor for a major publishing house, found that her formerly free weekends were often used for reading manuscripts. Since she enjoyed her work, she didn't mind putting in extra time in the evenings or on weekends. She felt that she had the option to do so while her married colleagues had less "free time" after work, with spouses and families making demands on their time.

So it appears that single men and women can be superior employees, yet they continue to receive lower wages than their married colleagues. According to George Gilder (1974:14), "most businesses know that single men, regardless of their intelligence and credentials, tend to be less stable and resolute workers than married

men.'' He adds that "discrimination is not the bachelor's problem
. . . (it) is his own psychological and physical condition. He is his
own worst enemy.'' Gilder reflects the attitudes—and the policies—
of many companies.

It is not a predominance of women among the singles in the
work force that lowers the average wages for single persons as a
group. Between the ages of twenty-five and thirty-five, single men
and women earn about the same hourly wage (Bernard, 1972:34).
Singles are often treated in much the same way that women are
treated in business. Singles (and women) are classified as being less
committed to their occupations, so that they do not warrant the
same salaries as "committed" married male workers.

It is reasonable to speculate that, contrary to Gilder's assertions,
salary discrimination experienced by singles in some industries may
contribute to the greater degree of mental problems (noted in
Chapter 2), particularly among single men. Since the work role is
so central to male identity in our society, it is reasonable to expect
that single men, if discriminated against in salaries and for promo-
tions, might exhibit more mental health problems than their
married colleagues.

Robert Gould, a psychiatrist, argues in "Measuring Masculinity
by the Size of a Paycheck" that, in our society, money not only
equals success, but also equals masculinity. A number of men
equate money-making with a sense of masculinity. Gould (Pleck &
Sawyer, 1974:96) says "that a man is too often measured by his
money, by what he is 'worth'—not his worth as a human being,
but by what he is able to earn; how much he can command on
the 'open market'.'' To the extent that single men subscribe to this
traditional ethic, and to the extent that their salaries are lower, they
are likely to feel "less masculine" and to be regarded as such by
colleagues and others.

There are other reasons for salary differentials. One of the functions of the family in our economic system is to maintain the present
work force and to prepare the next generation of workers, equipped
with the skills and values necessary for them to become productive
workers. Also, as David Cooper (1970) suggests, the first place a

child learns about authority and hierarchy is through the relations that govern relationships within his or her family.

It is the task of the family, from society's perspective, to raise children who internalize hierarchical social relations and who discipline themselves. Since the family performs these functions which are crucial for maintaining current political and power arrangements, the family as a social unit is to be encouraged. Some of the encouragement comes through higher salaries to married male heads of families.

LOANS AND CREDIT

Applications for loans and for credit revealed a specific pattern of discrimination, particularly against women. In one case, a divorced woman in her thirties, with a good, steady job and no debts, was refused car financing. The salesman told her that her husband would have to cosign. When she explained to the salesman that there was no husband in her life, he suggested that she get her parent to cosign.

Several banks have been known to discriminate against single women seeking loans. (The recently opened First Women's Bank in New York City will seek to change that practice.) Other businesses are also reluctant to extend credit to single women. The head of a collection agency, when asked about the practice, said that single women are more likely not to repay debts and loans when they marry and change names and addresses. Single, divorced, and widowed women are regarded as less financially responsible than married people. Several companies with whom women held credit cards refused to let them change the cards over to their own names when their husbands died. Several single women were denied credit card privileges. While single and working, Elizabeth was denied a $300 loan at a bank that advertises "friendship," and she was refused a credit card by a major credit card company, even though she had no debts. Hopefully, the new laws forbidding sexual discrimination regarding loans and credit will change these practices.

HOUSING

Nationwide, between the ages of fourteen and twenty-four, ninety per cent of single women and single men live with their relatives. Of those not living with relatives, about three per cent live alone. In the twenty-five to twenty-nine age group, fifty-one per cent of the men and forty-three per cent of the women still live with relatives. In the thirty to thirty-four year old group, fifty-one per cent of the men and forty-six per cent of the women live alone or with non-relatives (Bernard 1975:587-593). Age is clearly related to the physical move away from home.

In our sample of students (the Younger Sample) sixty-five per cent lived with their parents. (There are no dormitories at the college.) Sixteen per cent lived alone, six per cent lived with a same-sex roommate, and about nine per cent lived with an opposite-sex roommate. In contrast, none of the respondents in the Older Sample lived with their parents. About half of them lived alone and half with a roommate.

While most of the housing in the United States has been built for families (two adults and several children), there has been a steady increase over the last five years in the number of single persons maintaining their own households. Households headed by persons living alone or with non-relatives accounted for about forty-six per cent of the total household increase between 1970 and 1974. (About ninety per cent of the households headed by singles in 1974 consisted of one person living alone.) A majority of the three million new households in this category were headed by persons under thirty-five years of age (Glick, 1975).

Although more and more singles are households heads, they experience problems in finding housing. Several reported landlords preferring married couples to single persons because landlords and superintendents feared the noise and the amount of traffic that a single person and his friends would generate. One single woman said: "The manager told me that too many men would be going in and out of the apartment. Women need men to pay their rents for them. What if you get pregnant and can't work?" She told him to get lost and did not take the apartment.

On the other hand, there are landlords, builders, and real estate people who have combined their political and economic resources to establish residential and commercial areas that will attract young people of appropriate means. Census data indicate that a majority of the singles population is concentrated in very large cities and in specific areas of such cities. In his analysis of American youth Richard Flacks (1971) reports that a majority of college and post-college youths live in "youth ghettos." Although Haight-Ashbury in San Francisco, some sections of Santa Barbara, and New York City's Greenwich Village provide the most dramatic examples of "youth ghettos," each big city has them.

Some singles housing has resulted from urban renewal programs that have resulted in the urban removal of working-class and poor white ethnics and blacks. As their tenements and walk-ups are torn down, modern, efficient high-rise and high-price buildings are erected. Since only middle- and upper-income people can now afford the new rents, many of the new tenants are single college graduates who are willing (though not always able) to pay the rents in order to live near other singles, near theaters and first-run movie houses—in short, to be "where the action is."

Within the last two years, at least four major housing complexes (in Houston, Los Angeles, Atlanta, and Minneapolis) have opened specifically for singles. The one in Atlanta houses over 2,000 singles in apartments, and it includes lounges, swimming pools, bars, bowling alleys—and lots of parties. In some cases, social directors are responsible for drumming up business and getting people involved. One complex hired a "house mother" to look after singles who were having a hard time adjusting.

Gerda Wekerle's study of a high-rise complex (1975) provides some interesting details: It is a complex housing approximately 6,000 residents in nine buildings on Chicago's North Side. Called Carl Sandburg Village, it is comprised of a homogeneous group, most of the tenants being well-educated, professional, single young adults. According to Wekerle, the complex attracted people because of the location (convenient to major entertainment and shopping centers), the reasonable rent, and the "high percentage of singles." Old neighborhoods were "too old and too quiet" and "there wasn't much going on." Nor were there enough young people. The residential complex offered a "pool of eligibles" for dating and mating. Most of the respondents dated about six other residents, and, altogether, knew about nine people living at Sandburg. Several met their spouses there. Wekerle reports that, although "most initial contacts were made in the halls and the elevators, residents also became acquainted at the pool, at the ski and tennis clubs, at various Sandburg functions, at the supermarket and at the bus stop." At the same time, fewer than one-half of the people interviewed had ever used any of the facilities, and at least half of the respondents complained that the pool and the tennis courts were too expensive and too crowded.

In summary, Wekerle suggests several major reasons why single men and women were attracted to Carl Sandburg Village and other, similar singles' complexes: primarily, the homogeneity of residents in terms of age, income, interests, and stage of their life cycle and the fact that there they could be with others who, like themselves, occupied a deviant status—namely, being unmarried. In brief, a majority of the people living in the complex were having more fun than they had living elsewhere.

THE SINGLES MARKET

Because singlehood is currently attractive to many people, for either a short period or for all of their lives, and because business enterprises tend to exploit trends, there is a singles market emerging. The emerging singles market may be exploitative, but it also offers greater opportunity for enjoying a single life style than ever before.

There is a continuing increase in the number and range of goods and services available in our society. The population is being nurtured by the consumer ethic: The way to personal happiness is through consumption; prestige accrues from owning goods and services.

Although the family occupies a central place in the consumption economy, in order for producers to maximize their sales, it is imperative that all potential consumers learn to consume. So the individual becomes the focus of advertising appeals and media messages. Since any specific market grows as the number of potential customers increases, the family is broken down into various consuming units: mother, father, son, grandmother, and so forth. Each person is a member of some segmented market and may be appealed to through various channels. It is no longer enough for a family to own goods; each member of the family must want to own his or her personal goods. A recent ad shows a husband and wife lying next to each other in bed, he watching his set and she watching hers. The message is: Own your own, and be self-sufficient with your own goods. Sharing and cooperation take a back seat to consumerism.

The last fifteen to twenty years have also been characterized by a move from mass markets to fragmentation of the mass market. Robert Myers (1972:327) cites one business executive who explains it as: ". . . four distinct lines of products, appealing to four segments of the buying public, give a choice of product to fit most needs—either emotional of practical. . . . It's the case of going after all of some of the market rather than some of all of it."

Two considerations have affected marketing. First, the increase in the number of young and old has increased specialized demands for products. Second, there has been an increase in services—in household maintenance, in utilities, medical care, travel, and recreation—which consume more of the consumer's dollars. The media has responded to market segmentation through regional editions and split runs in consumer magazines, so that national advertisers can now expose specific products to specific markets and regions. Moreover, according to *Business Horizons* (1972:332): "Air media, spot television and radio advertising is rising. This also appeals to segmented ethnic or income groups via FM or foreign-language stations."

Singles have been identified by Eugene Gilbert of Gilbert Youth Research (1972:73) as part of the Youth Market. The eighteen to twenty-five year olds are:

subjected to . . . economic pressure. Young persons are forced to find a position that offers them opportunity. Most of them are anxious to settle down, build a home and raise a family. They are willing to try many new ventures and experiments until they find exactly what they are looking for. They experience complete buying power on their own without any consideration other than their income.

Every year, over two and one-half million young people enter this economic pressure for the first time. These people represent new sales potential for manufacturers. They start buying products for the first time and continue for the remainder of their lives. They are willing and anxious to experiment not only with positions, but also with merchandise. They are open-minded and are willing to try anything once that will help them or satisfy them.

Gilbert concludes that:

Today's Youth Market is an interesting potential for all wide-awake manufacturers. The important thing to remember is that, in order to reach them, it is necessary to understand them.

Two important aspects of the youth market are the singles industry and the marriage market, which include clients from eighteen to eighty, and which represent about $50 billion in annual sales.[1] In this market are products aimed directly at singles and more universal products for which singles represent a part of the total consumer group. Club Mediterranee vacations and single ski weekends in Colorado are aimed directly at the unmarried group. While ads for Pepsi Cola and Virginia Slims cigarettes may appear to be aimed at singles, they appeal to all young men and women, single or not.

The fact that a growing proportion of singles have a sizeable discretionary income, and that singles are probably less motivated to save, makes them an appealing market. Most singles do not have the pressure of mortgage payments, of feeding and educating children, paying property taxes, or building nest eggs. On the other hand, most singles do face higher income taxes, the higher cost of urban living, of singles housing, single-unit packaging, and single supplements for vacation packages.

One reason for capturing the singles market is the trade-up dictum. Advertising people know that the two-door Ford Pinto the

---

[1]Natalie Allon and Diane Fishel (1973) provide an interesting examination of singles' bars, an important segment of the singles industry.

single person buys today has a tendency to become the five-door Ford wagon he or she buys when married and living in the suburbs. It's important to establish brand loyalty early.

One of the major products being sold to singles is marriage. In *The Eternal Bliss Machine* (1974), Marsha Seligson describes a $7 billion industry. By October 1975, the bridal market had increased to $8 billion per year (*Bridal Trends,* October, 1975). Marketing projections suggest that newlyweds will continue to be "heavy consumers well into the 21st century. It's the 'hot market' and has been a major subject at store presidents' meetings."

More than $2 billion dollars per year are spent on wedding receptions alone. Forty per cent of the total jewelry business is based on engagements and weddings—a 1.6 billion dollar market. Some eighty per cent of the first-time weddings are formal, and ninety-six per cent have receptions. Almost all newlyweds take a trip following their weddings. Over $750 million is being spent on honeymoons: Honeymooners spend an average of $1,396 on trips outside the United States and about $833 on trips within the United States.

During the first year of marriage alone, young brides and grooms are spending an average of $4,500 on home furnishings, accounting for one out of every eight dollars being spent on home furnishings. They buy seventy-three per cent of all stainless flatware, sixty per cent of all sterling flatware and fifty-nine per cent of all fine china. Brides spend over half a billion dollars on lingerie each year—three and a half times as much as the average woman. The marriage industry appears to be doing well. There will be some 4,612,000 weddings in 1976 (*Bridal Trends,* October, 1975). *Modern Bride* magazine continues to carry more pages of advertising per issue than any other magazine in the United States (*Advertising Age:* November, 1974).

So it is important to the market place to keep the institution of marriage alive, not only because of the investment in marriage itself, but because, once wed, the consumer becomes part of the young-married market, and then of the young-parent market. For years, *Redbook* magazine has based its advertising solicitation on the eighteen to thirty-five-year-old young-parent market, claiming that to advertise in *Redbook* is to reach the heavy consumers.

Many marketing appeals are directed to finding a mate. Whether it is for an alluring cologne or a bottle of whisky, the needs of single people for self-worth and meaningful relationships are being exploited through merchandising. Advertising is often aimed at attracting members of the opposite sex. *Cosmopolitan* magazine revamped its format to attract just such advertising—and sold a phenomenal 1,389 pages of ads in eleven months of 1974 (*Advertising Age,* November, 1974). *Cosmopolitan's* place in the top four magazines for advertising revenue came only after its format was revamped to attract single women looking for a mate—and, naturally, to attract advertisers who wished to appeal to those women.

The fact that singles bars, singles clubs, and packaged singles vacations have become big business not only indicates that there is a vast singles market to be exploited, but may be contributing to the increased number of singles choosing to remain single. There is simply more to fill their lives as singles, and greater opportunity to participate in activities with other singles.

So, while there are positive aspects to singles marketing, industries continue to play upon the insecurities of the group in general. In fact, a recent trend in marketing uses fear- and anxiety-arousing appeals—appeals which are most effective for those who do not initially see themselves as part of the market for the product. For instance, a new twist on the fear of loneliness is the videodating service.

For about $75 for three months' membership, clients tape a four-minute session during which they talk about themselves, about their interests and careers, and about what they are looking for in the opposite sex. Each client views the tapes of others and choses those he or she would like to have view his or her own tape. It's a system that takes the anxiety out of meeting others; and it is also a system that greatly exploits that anxiety.

Increasingly, singles are seeking to be defined as responsible adults in an adult world, as peers among their peers. To do this, they must be cognizant of the ways others—including institutions—relate to them, and, sometimes, attempt to exploit them.

Chapter 4
Single Adults and Their Parents

From both of our samples, it is evident that parents are the major source of pressure toward marriage. For most parents, marriage appears to be the natural arrangement; other options don't exist. To remain single is not only different, but deviant. It is through socialization, "the process by which individuals acquire the knowledge, skills and dispositions that enable them to participate as more or less effective members of groups and society" that we learn family roles (Orville Brim in Brim & Wheeler, 1966). Most parents learned to accept marriage through their own socialization, and are attempting to pass the marriage value on to their children.

Through socialization, we internalize the attitudes, goals, and values of others. Our roles emerge out of contact with others: We take the roles of others by putting ourselves in their place. We reflect on ourselves by judging, or by attempting to judge, how others judge us; then we adopt the attitudes others have toward us and behave in accordance with those attitudes. We become finely tuned, especially to the wishes and preferences of those up upon whom we depend; and, in the early years, it is always the mother—whether biological or surrogate—upon whom we depend most. Through roles, identity is socially bestowed, socially sustained, and socially transformed (Berger: 1963).

In addition to the most obvious roles of father, mother, firstborn son, or youngest sibling, families construct more specialized roles for their members: the organizer, the scapegoat, the "good kid," the "bad kid," the achiever, the failure, the athlete, the intellectual, the clown, the victim, the mental case, the psychiatric nurse, and so forth. Children are assigned parts to play in the family drama.

In *Pathways to Madness,* Jules Henry (1972) describes the Portman family, with whom he lived, and the interaction between Mr. and Mrs. Portman and their son, Pete. Mr. Portman relates to Pete with roughness and toughness. "He expresses his love for his son through throwing him around, punching him in the belly and imitating a devouring animal. Mrs. Portman either ignores Pete or humiliates him by calling him a 'human garbage pail.' " Alternating between punching bag and garbage pail, Pete fulfills his assigned family role.

In their classic study of the family, R. D. Laing and Aaron Esterson (1970) show the cross currents of affection, hatred, and indifference in families that "script" children to become "insane." These are powerful examples of the process by which people learn roles in their families—roles that stay with them for a long time.

One of our interviewees was expected by her parents to be the entertaining, witty, accomplished maiden aunt who would be available to her sisters' children, and who, later on, would look after her aging parents. But most people are expected to marry a person regarded by (or even selected by) the family as appropriate. Family scripts are often so effective that we come to accept them as our own and do not bother to question their origins. Often, the scripts reflect predominant social values of the dominant culture, such as "You should marry a nice doctor and settle down." The very person selected as a mate is often a part of the family script.

Often the dialogues that develop over the details of courting and marriage (proper courting procedures, worthy candidates) are diversionary tactics that obscure the alternatives to marriage. Marriage messages include whom to marry; the time to marry (for example, after college); where to marry (the local church, with the family clergyman performing the ceremony); even how the wedding is to be staged (formal with the bride in white and the groom in tuxedo).

Karen recalled that, in the spring of 1971, after considerable agonizing over whether or not to marry, she decided to take the plunge. At first, she and her fiancee wanted to arrange the ceremony in a favorite spot of theirs in the wooded area of the college campus. They wanted a friend of theirs to perform a simple ceremony with a few close friends and their parents in attendance. Her mother objected to the plans as "too weird"; then his mother objected to the small number of guests being invited. Two weeks later, the mothers got together to talk about the wedding. After two more weeks, the mothers had constructed a wedding invitation list numbering close to one hundred persons. Exhausted at doing battle with the mothers, Karen resigned from dealing with the wedding at all and handed the arrangements over to her parents and future in-laws.

Most of the arguments are based on the parents' (and often, the childrens') assumption that marriage is desirable, appropriate and a "given." At age forty-five Travis had gone through two marriages. Of his marriages, he said:

Yes, of course I would be married. I desperately wanted to get married. It was expected by my family and it was never thought of as a choice, any more than college and a career in business were choices. Things were never put in terms of *are* you going to be married, but in terms of *when* you get married. . . .

What Travis said was echoed time and again by other respondents. The message was conveyed in various ways, but the basic content was the same: Parents were pressuring their single children to marry—and, moreover, to marry "well." For men, the message sometimes took the variant of pressure to establish a "good" career which would lead to a "good" marriage.

While both men and women felt parental pressure to marry and to marry "well," the women felt the pressure more. And their parents used several methods to send the messages.

In Maureen's experience:

> My mother used to send me clippings every time somebody got married, had children, stuff like that. When I moved in with Bill, she expressed disappointment . . . at my choice. When I was younger, she used to talk about all that romantic stuff with the long, white dress and the wedding in the garden, with the rhododendron in bloom. I still have the pressure inside me. I missed out on something for not going through that.

Although Maureen still clung to the fantasy of marriage, and to that extent still responded to parental pressure, she did express with clarity her conflict with the pressures put upon her.

> My mother's major concern was with status and prestige. He had to be a professional, a doctor, lawyer, professor . . . presentable, with a promising future. Not unlike Bill, the man I lived with for about three years. Before Bill, I thought I would never be able to live with anyone. After I had been living with him for a while, I started thinking about whether or not I wanted to get married. I could always think of better reasons for not marrying. Wanting to get married has a lot to do with the old propaganda: with security, status, the status of being a married woman. There are some things that are very hard about being a single woman. But I always was suspicious of those feelings. . . . I don't know that I will get married. I don't know whether or not I will really, really want to.

PREPARATION FOR MARRIAGE

The strong pressure for girls to marry is reflected in their fantasy lives. Our women respondents reported that, as youngsters, they talked about weddings, "good catches," children, and married life. At ages fourteen through sixteen, the men fantasized being in love with movie actresses and a few talked to their high school girlfriends about the number of children they would have; but for most, marriage was a foreign topic, and the marriages of older boys they knew seemed inconceivable.

On the whole, girls do considerably more rehearsing for the eventuality of marriage—a fact that is reinforced by children's toys for girls—bride dolls, doll houses, and the like.

One woman reported:

> I fantasized about marrying Paul McCartney, and my friend fantasized about marrying Ringo Starr. It would be a very elaborate wedding, and they would all play music after the wedding, while we danced around.

Said another respondent,

> I always thought that I would meet someone and settle down in a brownstone in the Village and have kids. I would still be political, would make crafts, and we would have a house on Fire Island for the summers. At the same time, my friends and I talked about having affairs on the side.

When Elizabeth Douvan and Joseph Adelson asked girls about their fantasies, some seventy-six per cent reported daydreaming about marriage. "For the large majority of girls, the common fantasy of marriage and family follows closely the lines of the popular image" (1966:233) which is the middle-class pattern. Girls want relationships "based on mutual love, respect, consideration and shared interests in which the husband cooperates in the home (1966:234).

When Douvan and Adelson (1966:235) asked students in a leading women's college to write short essays on how they would be living in the next ten years, a majority of the women reported a future that included:

(1) Marriage to a successful professional man or junior executive.
(2) Three or more children.
(3) A home in the suburbs.
(4) Daily activities including chauffeuring, shopping, and food preparation.
(5) A family income of $20,000 a year or more.
(6) A station wagon.
(7) Membership in community organizations.

Of some 14,000 college women surveyed in the late 1960s, a homogeneous fantasy projection emerged. Goals included marriage, an affluent life style, home ownership, a family life in the suburbs, two to four children, and at least two cars. Although careers were a consideration, motherhood and wifehood took precedence. Their desire was for mates of similar or higher social class, from similar ethnic and educational backgrounds (Stein: 1969).

Despite the fact that there have been changes in life styles in our society, the future-life fantasies of youngsters have changed surprisingly little in the last several decades.

When our Younger Sample of college students, was asked to describe their life situation in 1985, most included marriage, children, their own home—either in the city or in the suburbs—one or two cars, and a reasonably affluent life style. The answers cut across ethnic, racial, and income lines to evidence a fairly universal set of goals.

The fact that fantasy goals have not altered significantly attests to the strength of an early socialization which includes idealizing marriage and the family. Despite their reservations or outright criticism of the family, including their own families, most of the men and women in the Younger Sample felt that marriage was an institution that held hope for the future.

Over thirty years ago, Alan Bates (1942) reported that most children experience some direct parental influence in mate selection. At that time, sons reported that parental influence was brought to bear by their fathers in about forty-nine per cent of the cases, and by mothers in about seventy-nine per cent of the cases. Fathers influenced their daughters' choices of mates in some two-thirds of the cases, and mothers in almost every case. (Bates: 1942)

According to J. Richard Udry (1974), case history material from counselors' files indicated that parents participated in numerous ways in mate selection, including their choice of residential neighborhoods, schools for their children, and social club memberships —all of which consciously controlled the social companions available to their children.

Sometimes pressure to marry is direct, and sometimes it is quite subtle. Either way, it tends to continue to be a pressure as long as children remain single.

In Kim's experience:

> Mother wanted me to get the best, finest and richest man. . . . She stopped me from swimming regularly because she thought my arms would become deformed and no man would want me. . . . To make sure I would be a good catch, I was given a dowry of silver, which couldn't be used because it was too soft.

Barbara, now twenty-six, has felt the pressure from her parents more recently. There are scheduled telephone calls from her mother providing the latest family gossip, followed by the inevitable parting shot: "So, what's new with you? Have you met anyone nice? You know you're not getting any younger. . . ."

Phil's father periodically raises the question of grandchildren. "They'll bring joy and pleasure; your mother loves children, and they keep the family line going."

BARGAINING

Bargaining tends to form a major mode of interaction between parents and children. Often, money and emotional leverage are the weapons in the fight. While parents may still have a monopoly on the purse, the young adult is well schooled in family patterns of provocation and reproach. The Younger Sample respondents reported minor skirmishes around the use of the family car, curfews, visiting relatives, and living off-campus. Conflict appeared to intensify over such issues as the choice of an academic major and career decisions—including the desire to "knock around for a while to gather some life experience." Cold war conditions of co-existence seemed to prevail. Although most parents and children know just how far the other will go and do not get into open fights, the tensions are there. Nancy, of the Older Sample, recalls the years immediately following her graduation from college: "I knew that my parents would not approve of a lot of the things I was doing, so I was careful not to rub their noses in it. I never asked for financial help to support me in my life style." It also appears that many parents ease certain pressures on their older children, fearing that too much pressure will cause the children to break off contact with the family altogether.

THE MOVE TOWARD INDEPENDENCE

Parents appear to remain arbiters of experience and decision making long after such influence is appropriate. How long *is* appropriate?

Young adults tend to need some financial support and emotional support from their families in order to get their own lives started. An adolescent is not an oversized child but a young, immature adult, one who needs both independence and support in order to develop on his own terms. As the adolescent matures into a young adult, he becomes less dependent on his parents, and, presumably, the amount of contact between parent and child diminishes. Our data suggests this to be true.

Sixty-five per cent of the Sample A, the Younger Group, lived with their parents while none of the Older Singles Sample lived with their parents. Most of the Younger Sample had frequent contact with their parents (about once a week), while most of the Older Sample members had infrequent contact with their parents. Eighty-five per cent of the Younger Sample reported receiving emotional support from their parents, but only about twenty per cent of Sample B reported such parental support. Among several of the Older Sample respondents, strong disagreement over the issues of marriage and life style precipitated a decline or break in contact with their parents.

For both groups, friendships outside of one's family have gained importance in providing emotional support. More than ninety per cent of both samples reported receiving emotional support from friends.

Typically, the first step toward independence is the physical move away from home to school or college, to a job in a new city—or to an early marriage.

If the parent continues to have power over the young adult into his late teens and early twenties, it is because the young adult has not exercised independence and continues to see his parents as overriding authorities. Just as letting go is difficult for parents, the exercise of independence is difficult for the young adult. Moreover, our culture and our institutions tend to perpetuate dependence on parents and to stress parental power over teenage children.

Society also tends to induce and reinforce guilt feelings for children of any age who strive to go their own way—feelings that are more apparent in those single adults who are decidedly going "their own way."

Chapter 5
Sex and Singles

In the mid-sixties, Helen Gurley Brown wrote *Sex and the Single Girl.* Suddenly, single women not only could but should have sex lives. At about the same time, Hugh Hefner was publishing the ongoing *Playboy Philosophy,*[1] and Ian Fleming was creating what was perhaps the ultimate single swinger in James Bond, the double agent who indulged in fast, expensive games; fast, expensive cars—and "fast, expensive" women.

The Old Maid and the Mamma's Boy stereotypes of single people were being replaced, to a large degree, by a new stereotype—the swinging single.

Stereotypes prescribe behavioral and attitudinal norms for group members, provide recruitment guidelines, influence people to become members of a group, and instruct outsiders to the group

[1]It is interesting to note that, even in the midst of a "sexual revolution," the double standard applied. The single girl was to use sex in pursuit of a mate, whereas the single man was to use sex in pursuit of pleasure.

as to how they should regard the insiders. Stereotypes are power-ful images, indeed.

Stereotypes provide *ideal* roles of behavior, and they abound in all spheres of social life. They may or may not coincide with reality. Institutions often foster stereotypes in order to control reactions to the institution. For example, some colleges are stereo-typed as prestigious, elite, and exclusive in order to attract certain kinds of students.

The swinger stereotype for singles attracts some to the group and repulses others. For instance, the female swinger is supposed to be popular; she's appealing to the opposite sex. She's "together." But what if she's not? What if she is genuinely terrified of sex? She feels pressure to pretend to be someone she isn't. With each new attempt to experience sex, she is trapped by the expectation of performance—sexual performance—on demand. Perhaps that part of her life isn't "together" yet. And what about the swash-buckling single male? If the whole evening with a woman is about going to bed, his expected "performance" at the end of the evening may loom large in the script. What if he's not ready for the con-quest, or what if his current needs are other than sexual? And what if the evening were not to end in sex? If that sounds somehow deviant, it's a measure of how affected we are by the stereotype.

The fact is that single people, being human, have the same problems with sex, intimacy, and tenderness as anyone else. Neither the married nor the single state guarantees easy solutions to any of life's problems. In fact, to the extent that the stereotype of the swinging single has been expanded to James Bond proportions— to proportions beyond actual achievable roles—the single person may feel a range of negative emotions in attempting to live up to that role. The single person might feel rejection, fear, hostility, and ineptitude instead of sensuality and satisfaction. Some single people might even avoid situations where their ideal role is severely challenged and look, instead, for other roles to occupy.

The ideal role of the swinger represses feelings of anxiety, doubt, and incompetence because it is important that he or she maintain an image of invulnerability; yet it can be difficult for a person to grow if he or she is not in touch with real feelings. The swinger role tends to attract people who feel they can manage it, whether or not they really can. Other singles want to explore their sexuality and to experiment with sustaining relationships while retaining their independence, but they feel that the fast, swinging singles scene does not meet those needs. They would rather not participate in the swinging singles life style, but find it difficult to find alternatives.

One of the characteristics of the swinging singles life-style is casual sexual encounters. Although almost all of our respondents had had experiences they could characterize as "one night stands," their feelings about their experiences were ambivalent. For some men and women, the sexual experience was "fun," "great," "enjoyable," "satisfying," and "close." For others, it was "not very satisfying," "awkward," or "sad." Casual sexual encounters could be enjoyable at one time, less enjoyable at others. To a twenty-six year old woman who had recently broken up with a man: "There are no hard and fast rules. Something about one night stands repulses me. I guess it's the attitude around sex. It's expected rather than anticipated. Many men are too immature. A turn-down is met with feelings of rejection."

Although more men than women reported that they enjoyed casual sexual encounters, some men were "scared," or "lost interest after a one-night stand." Both men and women respondents indicated that casual sexual contacts were better when it was clear to both parties that the relationship was casual—that there would be no strings attached. The experience turned sour when they expected a follow-up to the casual encounter and none occurred.

LOVE

The most readily available alternative to casual sexual encounters has been romantic love—love that will precipitate marriage, that will, in turn, precipitate sex. What, then, is love?

In 1694, the *Ladies' Dictionary* defined love like this: " 'Tis very much like light, a thing that everybody knows, and yet none can tell what to make out of it." Our understanding of love hasn't changed much in the last 300 years. Listen to popular songs and you will hear love defined as a commodity, as a compulsion, as a master-slave relationship, as sexual performance, as security, as attraction—and as a host of other things.[2]

Richard Udry sampled definitions of love from textbooks on marriage and the family and from the writings of psychologists, psychiatrists, philosophers, ministers, poets, and other "experts"; he reported a conglomeration similar to one produced when he sampled a group of college students.

Table IV
The Meaning of Love: Definitions of
College Students

Feeling of Attraction	40%
Companionship & Compatability	20%
Giving	20%
Security	17%
Other	3%

Source: J. Richard Udry, *The Social Context of Marriage.* New York: Lippincott, 1974:132.

We tend to ignore the dubious logic of calling a wide range of emotions and responses—including hate, control, dominance and denial—love. In fact, many Americans say they marry for love. The underlying reasons may include a strong emotional commitment, economic gain, status striving, a desire to leave home or to get away from parents, escape from loneliness, keeping up with the crowd or sexual gratification—but it's generally called "love."

SEX AS SCRIPTED BEHAVIOR

The recent work by William Simon and John Gagnon (1974) challenges the long-held Freudian view that psychosexual energy in

[2]Some mid-seventies examples of love in popular music: Coupled love ("Two of Us"—Paul McCartney); tripled love ("Triad"—Graham Nash); love as a commodity ("Shopping Around"—Smokey Robinson); love as compulsion and addiction ("Don't You Want Somebody to Love"—Grace Slick); love as master-slave relationship ("Dominance-Submission"—the Blue Oyster Cult); love as performance ("Sex Machine"—James Brown); confusion about love ("Both Sides Now"—Judy Collins).

the form of libido is essential—"a biological constant"—and that sexual development is a continuous contest between biological drives and cultural restraint. Simon and Gagnon (1974:146) suggest that, contrary to the Freudian dictate that there are "sexual elements in nonsexual behavior and symbolism," the reverse is the case: namely, "that sexual behavior can often express and serve nonsexual motives." They suggest that sexual behavior is "scripted behavior," not an expression of primordial drive. We thus learn sexual behavior as we learn other behavior:

> through scripts that, in this case, give the self, other persons and situations erotic abilities or [erotic] content. Desire, privacy, opportunity and propinquity with an attractive member of the opposite sex are not, in themselves, enough. In ordinary circumstances, nothing sexual will occur unless one or both actors organize these elements into an appropriate script.

According to Simon and Gagnon's research, about one-half of all adults reported that they had engaged in some form of sex play between the ages of eight and thirteen; relatively few experienced active sex before adolescence.

In our society, to learn about sex is primarily to learn about guilt. "An important source of guilt in children comes from the imputation to them, by adults, of sexual appetites or abilities they may or may not have, but that they learn, however imperfectly, to pretend they have" (Simon and Gagnon, 1974:148). The crucial period of childhood is important not because of sexual experiences, but because of "nonsexual developments that will provide the names and judgments for later encounters with sexuality" (1974: 149). Simon and Gagnon feel that for adults rather than "sexual needs affecting other adult concerns, the reverse may be true: adult sexual activity may become that aspect of a person's life most often used to act out other needs." (1974:156).

ATTITUDES TOWARD SEX

When sociologists examine sexual activity, they generally differentiate between attitudes and behavior. Attitudes are learned;

they are feelings that usually have a negative or positive weighting and lead to a generally predictable response. Behavior is action—a response to some stimulus. In some cases, attitudes are accurate predictors of behavior; in other cases, they are not.

Lucile Duberman (1974) identifies a basic contradiction in American values regarding premarital sex. On one hand, compared to other societies, we allow our children a relatively substantial amount of information regarding sex and sexual techniques—and a good deal of privacy. Our culture abounds with symbols of sexuality to which our children are exposed, primarily through movies, books, and television. On the other hand, parents prohibit their children from having premarital intercourse, and the culture still advocates sexual abstinence prior to marriage. Our children are placed in a cultural double-bind. There must be no premarital experience, yet we permit many opportunities for it to occur.

CHANGES IN SEXUAL ATTITUDES AND BEHAVIOR

In two national samples conducted by the Elmo Roper Agency, one in 1937 and the other in 1959, men and women were asked how they felt about premarital intercourse. In all that time span, there was virtually no change in attitude. More than half of the men and women felt that neither party to marriage should have engaged in premarital sex (Hunt, 1974:114).

Sexual attitudes and behavior appear to be changing radically. Morton Hunt, in *Sexual Behavior in the 1970s,* made what he regarded as the most extensive survey on sexual attitudes and behavior since Kinsey; and he reported dramatic shifts in attitudes toward greater permissiveness in sexual ideas and sexual experiences. While only twenty-two per cent of the adults surveyed by Roper in 1959 indicated approval for premarital sex, Hunt's survey conducted in 1972 indicated that some sixty-five per cent of adults expressed approval of premarital sex for men and some fifty per cent expressed approval for women. The approval depended upon the degree of affection or emotional involvement between the partners (Hunt, 1974).

In 1953, Kinsey reported that one-third of the single women in his sample had experienced sex by age twenty-five. Hunt reported in 1972 that some seventy-five per cent had experienced sex by age twenty-five. In Kinsey's report, of those who had married before age twenty-five about one-half had experienced premarital sex— similar to Hunt's data—but, among the youngest women in the sample, the figure for premarital sex was eighty per cent. Among non-college men, Kinsey reported that two-thirds had had premarital sex by age seventeen; Hunt reported that about three-fourths of the men had premarital sex by age seventeen. And, among college males, in 1950, about one-fourth had engaged in sex prior to marriage; in 1972, about one-half had engaged in premarital sex.

In September and October 1975, *Redbook* magazine published a report conducted by Robert and Amy Levin on the sexual experiences of 100,000 American women.[3] Ninety per cent of the women surveyed who were under twenty-five years of age said that they had had premarital intercourse, figures which represent a dramatic shift over the past twenty year period.

Table V
Changes in Premarital Sex Behavior, 1953–1975.

Year Report Issued:	Source:	Sample:	Percentage of women under 25 having experienced premarital intercourse
1953	Kinsey	8,000	33%
1974	Hunt	2,000	75%
1975	Levin and Levin	100,000	90%

[3]Although the *Redbook* survey sample did not parallel the population (nine of ten were married, compared to seven of ten in the population, and it favored better-educated and financially secure women), it is significant in that it represents the largest number of women ever questioned by a research group.

The *Redbook* survey also indicated that the more recent the marriage, the greater the probability of sex prior to marriage.

Table VI
Change in Premarital Sex Behavior

Year of Marriage	Percentage of women having intercourse prior to marriage
Before 1964	69%
Between 1964 and 1969	81%
Between 1970 and 1973	89%
From 1974 to 1975	93%

Source: Robert Levin and Amy Levin, "The Redbook Report: A Study of Female Sexuality," *Redbook Magazine,* 1975.

The Levins report that women are having their first sexual experience earlier than did their mothers. Fifty per cent of women high school graduates had sexual intercourse between their sixteenth and seventeenth birthdays, and one-half of women college graduates had first intercourse between ages eighteen and nineteen.

About one-third of the women in the *Redbook* survey reported having had sexual relations with men other than their husbands while they were married. Statistics indicated that the longer a woman had been married, the greater was the likelihood that she would engage in extra-marital sexual relations.

The results of several polls indicate that there is a generation gap in attitudes toward premarital sex. A *New York Daily News* poll conducted in late 1975 showed that sixty percent of the eighteen to thirty-four-year-olds interviewed approved of unmarried couples living together whereas sixty-seven percent of those fifty years old and over disapproved. (*Daily News,* Dec. 15, 1975:5). James Ramey (1976) provides further evidence. He cites a recent Cornell University study by Eleanor Macklin asking both parents and students if they had known any couples that lived together. While "a third of the parents indicated that they knew their own children had cohabited . . . , two-thirds of those children reported that either they or their siblings had cohabited. . . . Since two-thirds of the parents disapproved of premarital sexual activity, whereas two-thirds of the students thought it was all right, it is understandable that most families are not likely to exchange information or points of view in this highly charged area."

According to our Younger Sample, seventy-three percent of the fathers and eighty-three per cent of the mothers disapproved of sex prior to marriage whereas seventy-nine per cent of the sons and daughters approved of sex prior to marriage. In our survey and in others, the difference in attitude between generations is more strongly apparent than the difference in attitudes between the sexes.

Table VII
"As far as you know, how does/did each of the following feel about premarital sex?"

	Father	*Mother*	*Self*	*Friends*
Disapproves strongly	55%	56%	4%	1%
Disapproves somewhat	18%	27%	7%	6%
Doesn't care	4%	1%	10%	13%
Approves somewhat	7%	9%	36%	27%
Approves strongly	4%	4%	43%	54%

Source: Sample A (N = 125)

Despite their parents' opposition to sex before marriage, seventy-one per cent of our Sample A respondents had had one or more sexual experiences.

SINGLES AND THE MEANING OF SEX

For singles, the meaning of sex evokes a wide range of responses. When asked, "What does having sex mean to you?", the men in both of our samples replied: "Something I enjoy doing and feel is important," "communication," "orgasm," "monogamy," "tenderness," "just feeling good about the person," "being human," "love," "being turned on," and "ecstasy." For some, the meaning of sex varied with mood and with the person they were with. For many, the nature of the relationship provided an important context for the meaning of sex.

For a twenty-four year old man, sex meant "being in love and loving—close interactions, physical sharing and caring for one another." For a twenty-three year old man, sex was "a private experience that I enjoy as a way of solidifying a relationship." And, for a twenty-five year old man, it was "getting it on with someone for a physical and emotional release. When love is involved, that's an added attraction." In our samples, it was the younger men who were more likely to mention love and affection.

For our women respondents, sex depended "upon how I feel about my partner," and upon "depth of feelings," "its context in the relationship," and "how good I am feeling about myself." Sex was "enjoyment—if I am really there." For some, sex was "tenderness and cuddling," "closeness," "love," "being turned on physically." Some were more interested in getting to know their partners before engaging in sex.

Doris pointed to some of the complexities involved:

> I can use sex as an obsession and worry about whether or not I'll find someone. What sex is, is physical contact between two people. I can use it to throw a monkey wrench into a situation, or can cut out on the experience and just space out. I can also use sex in a provocative way to seduce a guy or scare him off.

As with the men, the younger women were more likely to speak of love and romance in association with sex. For a nineteen year old, sex was "a union between two people deeply in love with each other who are compatible and share similar goals. They learn from and help each other." A twenty-four year old woman regarded sex as "enjoying a moment of excitation and passion with someone you love." For a twenty-one year old, "having sex with someone you care for is very important for a relationship and will make it stronger."

For a majority of our respondents, love and sex did not necessarily have to go together. Fewer than five per cent of the Older Sample and fewer than fifteen per cent of the Younger Sample felt that "one had to be in love or care for the other person deeply before having sex."

SEX AND SELF-ESTEEM

For sixty-three per cent of the men and women in the Younger Sample, the sexual experience increased their self-esteem, while it decreased self-esteem for twelve per cent. Twenty-five per cent said they were not affected either way. Similarly, sixty-nine per cent of the Younger Sample attributed sex to strengthening a relationship; nine per cent said it weakened the relationship; and, for twenty-two per cent, sex had no effect in the overall strength of the relationship.

Some men and women focused their responses on the physical pleasures of sex: "It's an intense pleasure." "Dynamite." "I feel better after making love." "It makes me feel human and desirable." For others, there appeared to be a close link between how they felt about themselves and their general mood on a given day and how they felt about sex.

Sue Ann said:

If I feel good, sex is almost always good and, if I feel bad, it's likely to be awful. Sometimes I can get out of the bad mood by feeling close to someone, but usually the mood stays there. It helps if I let myself talk it out . . . much depends on the experience, and who I am with.

For some of the women, particularly several divorcees who had had sex with only their husbands for a number of years, the prospect of having sex on the first date was anxiety-provoking. For Sarah, who was one week short of being a virgin bride, the possibility of men as potential sex partners after a six year, sexually exclusive marriage, was frightening. She recalled an anxiety attack on the day of a date that almost made her cancel it. Although she kept the date, the evening was difficult. She tried her best to make conversation and to be as charming as possible, but her insides were churning. Later, when she called a friend and talked about the experience, she began to realize just how frightened she had been. Her memories of first dates in high school and college had come rushing back with the emotions she had felt that evening.

POSSESSIVENESS AND EXCLUSIVITY

In many ways, we are taught to possess, control, and manipulate those we love, and jealousy is interwoven with our notions of romantic love. To return to Simon and Gagnon (1974), exclusivity is a culture-bound script. It is that part of the socialization process that insures the continuation of monogamy, commitment, marriage, and the family.

Early socialization pressures are toward exclusivity, and it can be difficult for a person who is trained for exclusive heterosexual relationships to learn to date and relate to more than one person of the opposite sex at a time. For example, Marion recalled that "when my boyfriend and I moved in together, we instantly became monogamous . . . just as if we were married. We were very much into each other."

Later, Marion broke up with her boyfriend and faced difficulty with multiple relationships:

> Initially, it was hard to see several people. I think it's because of our monogamous society. I dated people usually one at a time and then it expanded. Now I'm dating several people. I prefer that, actually. You get too dependent if you date one person. And if that person is dependent on you solely, it's hard on him. I think it's really an unfair way to relate. It places too many demands on somebody else.

All of the respondents in the Older Sample had current ongoing relationships with several persons of the opposite sex. Most of the respondents had regular contact with at least five persons of the opposite sex once every ten to fourteen days. Some of the relationships were sexual; some were not. Most people had at least one person of the opposite sex they met regularly without sexual involvement.

Those who had lived in exclusive relationships faced problems similar to those of their married counterparts. For Sandra, however, the change in her dating pattern was exciting:

> I have just begun to see men again, and am very excited about getting to know men as people all over again. In an exclusive relationship, I lost knowing how to relate to men.

Her excitement over new relationships seemed to help offset the tension of dealing with several relationships at the same time.

Most respondents felt that there were limits on how involved they could get with more than one person or a few persons—and that such limits were socially rather than psychologically defined. The limits stemmed from notions of monogamy or exclusivity and were reinforced by familial prohibitions on the number of strangers most children are allowed to interact with. The concepts of limited love and limited energy were felt to have been socially imposed. Joan, a divorcee, offered an analogy:

> I have two children, and the first child, when she was born, I thought, "I don't have enough love for another child. It's using up all of the capacity I've got." I thought in terms of a very limited capacity I guess, or at least, a capacity that was pretty well defined. When the second child was born, I found out that it expanded and there was more, and I had a feeling at that time there was probably a lot that was untapped. And it wasn't at all like I thought it was. And therefore, I—to extrapolate it onto your question—I really think that people have an almost unlimited capacity, limited only by time, and obligations of one sort or another, to have intense and good and satisfying relationships with a number of people. I don't think that you have only so much that you can give or love or enjoy.

Joan's experiences suggest that some unmarrieds have been able to move beyond their early socialization for exclusivity and enjoy multiple satisfying relationships.

SUMMARY

Since we are experiencing what appear to be changes in the national attitude toward sex among singles, and since there appears to be a corresponding change in sexual behavior among singles, there is some reality to the change in the stereotype of singles. However, as with all stereotypes, the swinging single typing fits only a portion of all singles—and even then, only a portion of the time. Like everyone else, singles may be caught up in scripted sexual behavior and may be limited by the stereotypes held by others.

"It can be a drag," said Jennifer.

Because I am single and have my own apartment, people expect me to behave in certain ways. It's very difficult to have platonic relationships with men, for instance. Men I work with—even family friends who are married and have families I have known for years—expect a sexual relationship from me. They almost expect all my relationships to be sexual. Sex is a great part of a relationship—when it's appropriate. It's just that it's not always appropriate. It can undermine some kinds of relationships—and enhance others.

The general confusion over love, sex, and exclusivity, affects singles as well as marrieds. However, some singles are discovering that their preferred life styles do not necessarily have to comply with the scripts written for them; and they are choosing to write scripts of their own—a difficult task.

Chapter 6
The Choice to Be Single

What are the needs of single people and which needs may or may not be satisfied by choosing to be single? How do individuals develop, grow, and change? What does the choice to marry or to stay single mean in the development of the individual? How do single people experience themselves in the world? What are the "pushes" and the "pulls" from parents, from society, and from within themselves that affect their choice?

There is a multiplicity of reasons for getting in and out of marriage. Our main concern in this chapter is to examine these pushes and pulls to see how they have influenced the group of men and women in Sample B who have chosen *not* to marry. The major assumption in our society is that to be single beyond one's mid-twenties indicates that either one has failed to find the right person, or that one is in an intermission between marriages. Our data indicate that, although some of the men and women we studied are single because they have not yet found a suitable mate, and although others have not married primarily because they were expected not to marry by their parents, there is an emerging group of men and women who have made a positive choice not to marry at this stage of their lives. While some of these men and women have experienced marriage or marriage-like exclusive relationships, they have decided that they prefer singleness.

The positive choice to stay single receives little cultural or institutional support in our society. For the respondents themselves, wanting to be single was a new experience, one that they were experimenting with for themselves. For them, at the time, to be single was better. For some, their feelings were relative to prior bad experiences of marriage. They felt more open in their single state than they had in prior cohabitations. Many had felt their needs for new experiences blocked and deadened by their marriage relationships. Respondents spoke time and again of patterns that revealed interpersonal contracts to ignore new experiences, to "settle down" and accept established patterns of interaction and relating. In these relationships, whether they were official marriages or not, there was an atrophy of new experiences and a lack of personal expansion. They felt themselves not as growing, expanding, and developing, but as stagnating, as bored or frustrated. For many, the contrast with their present lives is striking, and the single experience is for them a gratifying and a positive one. Their experiences suggest that the choice to be single can be a viable life choice.

Table VIII summarizes the major factors reported by respondents in the Older Sample regarding their decisions to marry, never to marry, or—once married or living with a lover—to separate. While each person's experiences, joys, and disappointments are unique, certain common patterns of experiences, pressures, and feelings emerge from our data. One way of seeing these common patterns is to report them as a series of pushes and pulls. Typically, persons we spoke to were propelled by some factors into marriage or marriage-like situations; subsequently, their motivations for marriage were overcome by their dissatisfactions, and the attractions of the single life were found more compelling. Pushes represent negative factors in a current situation while pulls represent attractions to a potential situation.

Table VIII
Pushes and Pulls Toward Being Married and Being Single

Toward Being Married	
Pushes (negatives in present situation)	*Pulls (attractions in potential situations)*
Pressure from parents	Approval of parents
Need to leave home	Desire for family
Fear of independence	Example of peers
Loneliness	Romanticization of marriage
Cultural expectations, socialization	Physical attraction
	Emotional attachment and love
Guilt over singlehood	Security, social status, prestige
No sense of alternatives	Sexual availability

Toward Being Single	
Pushes	*Pulls*
Restrictions within relationship:	Career opportunities
Suffocating one-to-one relationship, feeling trapped	Variety of experiences and plurality of roles
Obstacles to self-development	Self-sufficiency
Boredom, unhappiness, and anger	Sexual availability
	Exciting life style
Role playing and conformity to expectations	Freedom to change and mobility
Poor communication with mate	Sustaining friendships
Sexual frustration	Psychological and social autonomy
Lack of friends, isolation, loneliness	
Limited mobility and availability of new experiences	

The strength of these pushes and pulls is highly relative. They vary in intensity according to a number of factors. Pressures from parents to marry may be experienced very strongly by some and hardly at all by others. Some see being alone with great fear, and they seek a mate to fill the perceived void. Others seek friends

with whom to spend time. Physical attraction and emotional involvement can lead to marriage for some, to living together for
others, or can be enjoyed without a more permanent attachment
by still others. However, the same person experiences the same
pushes or pulls in different ways at different stages of his or her
life cycle. There is a roughly defined set of age categories that
helps shape people's relations to one another. People expect
different accomplishments and are prepared to accept different
behavior according to their age group (Turner, 1970:370). Philip
Slater (1970), Margaret Mead, (1970), Richard Flacks (1971) and
others have documented the confusing and contradictory elements
in the transition from adolescence to adulthood in American society.
With respect to marriage, however, there is a clear cultural imperative to marry in one's late teens or early twenties, although with
an increase in the number of high school graduates going on to
college, and with more women working, the age of first marriage
has risen. While the marriage imperative is stronger for women,
men are also expected to marry, at least by the time of their thirtieth
birthday.

   College or career may be used by some people to seek a mate,
and by others to develop relationships outside of the context of
marriage. Many people on college campuses are not able or do not
want to see alternatives to marriage. They, and others around
them, see the choice not to seek a mate as failure. The work experience provides an excuse for "settling down" for some, and
offers a promise of more varied and fuller experiences with other
people for others. Even people who experienced a pull toward
marriage, and found friends who supported them in their search
for a mate may have, at a later time in their lives, found greater
pulls toward a satisfying career, good work associations, more
friends, and more fun—all of which seemed more likely outside of
marriage. The cultural strength of the push to marry also varies
with time. In recent years, the attractiveness of marriage itself may
be diminishing. The growing divorce rate and the bad press marriage
has received has at least made more people wary of it. Single
persons today tend to be more cautious about taking that step than
were single persons ten years ago. More speak of open relationships, of greater freedom for both within marriage, and of greater
flexibility.

Perceiving and exercising choices and options in a situation influence the kind of decision that will be made. Experiences outside the familiar family pattern, available through college or work, may be used by some people to experiment with alternative styles of behavior or relationships, while others in the same external situation may not perceive or be able to try out options different from those envisioned by their parents. The capacity to make use of experience to expand one's range of choice stems in good measure from the development of empathy—that is, the capacity the person has to identify with and put himself in the place of another. According to Ralph Turner (1970:372): "Placing oneself in the position of the other and inferring attitudes, motives, and sentiments from that point of view makes the subtleties of human interaction possible." Cultural examples of very limited empathy for others abound, and, as Turner suggests, unless members of the family have had "sufficient experience with relevant others" to develop the capacity for empathy, the child will find it difficult to develop such capacity. Lack of empathy blocks appreciation for others and for alternative ways of living and responding to rules and cultural imperatives, including marriage. Age role, sex-role identity, the development of empathy, and the development of the conception of rules converge in the development of an identity. As Turner (1970:375) states it: "The identity can be no more complex than the elaboration of the individual's capacity for role-taking permits." That is, the capacity for empathy and the flexibility of age roles and sex-role identity are crucial for the development of a complex identity capable of seeing and exercising options and alternatives.

Most of our respondents spoke of the freedom and enjoyment which being single offered them. There are opportunities to meet and spend time with and develop relationships with a number of people, both men and women. For many, staying single is better than marriage. Susan, who had lived with a man for about a year, said that there's:

> . . . a hell of a lot more freedom than there would be either in marriage or an exclusive relationship. I like a lot of different people, and being single kind of affords the opportunity for getting to know and being friends with a lot of different people. No restrictions except the ones I happen to choose. They are not superimposed upon me by someone else's jealousy, for instance.

For some, like Mike, a lawyer, "It's not so much being single as it is not being married—not being in an exclusive relationship at all."

Some of the singles in our study experienced various pressures from others—work colleagues, family members, relatives. At twenty-eight, Brenda sometimes felt that she should either be married and be thinking about raising a family, or that she should be pursuing a professional career. The fact that neither course of action was succeeding had concerned her. Although she had little current contact with her parents, she still felt their pressure toward her marrying. On the other hand, because of the economic recession in her field, she had lost her job as an architectural designer and was currently unemployed. Although she did not plan to marry in the near future, she was concerned about what others would think. "When I tell some people I'm twenty-eight and not married they look at me like there's something wrong—they think I'm a lesbian. Some just feel sorry for me. What a drag."

Ellen illustrates the competing pushes and pulls inherent in the single status in our society.

> There's a part of me that sees being single as freedom, possibilities of meeting different kinds of people and having different kinds of relationships, which is the exciting part, and there is a whole part that looks at it as bull—where I'll ultimately end up lonely, where something is the matter with me because I'm not in love with somebody and somebody is not in love with me, whatever that means.

Ellen was also expressing the confusion and frustration of someone who feels that the alternatives are limited. Ellen's needs were obscured in the confusion.

The concern with appearances (How will others see me? What will they think?) is a major factor in the social pressure placed on people to marry. Earlier studies suggest that never to marry is a failure which reflects an individual's shortcomings and inadequacies. Singles are expected to adapt to a social context that rewards marriage and wherein "almost all major roles and related values are based on the assumption of marital experience." (Manford

Kuhn, 1955). Robert Bell (1975), in a discussion of Kuhn's work, suggests that certain characteristics, such as unattractiveness, are "a factor in *not being selected,* whereas hostile marriage attitudes refer to *not actively selecting.*"

Bell further states that "a person who is not actively seeking a mate has . . . withdrawn from the mate selection process." This description also applies to those respondents in Sample B who are not actively selecting a mate. They have exercised the choice not to do so. However, in contrast to Kuhn's findings, most of our respondents offered positive reasons for remaining single. Such factors as parent fixation, physical or health problems, unattractiveness, unrealistic romantic expectations, economic problems, conflict between marriage and career desires, and isolation from the dating market did not characterize any of our respondents. There did not appear to be a lack of proficiency in dealing with the dating/mating game, but rather a rejection of it as competitive, outmoded, and exploitative.

Negative attitudes toward marrige and its implied roles and responsibilities may be termed "pushes" away from marriage toward singlehood insofar as dissatisfaction motivates the search for an alternative. Our respondents reflected a spectrum of negative attitudes, mostly based on their own experience in a marriage or coresidential exclusive relationship. While most did not question the validity of marriage as an institution, the majority were quite certain that they would not choose to marry in the future. Several persons indicated that, although they felt some guilt about not being married because of pressures from family or married friends, they rejected marriage as a personal choice. The idea of a nonmarital exclusive relationship elicited more ambivalent feelings. A number of the respondents stated that they were open about this as an option for some future time—on a strictly tentative and experimental basis, however. All respondents emphasized that exclusivity at this time in their lives would constitute a critical limitation on their freedom and growth.

Indeed, the theme of marriage as a restriction and obstacle to human growth showed up as the strongest push in our study. It was often based on the attitude that one central relationship as an exclusive source of emotional support and social identity was both unrealistic and confining. In response to the question of why he chose to remain single, Tom said:

> When I was in an unofficial marriage with a woman, I would see only her and would be totally focused on her as the deciding factor of how my mood would be. It was a way of keeping myself out of having anything for myself and depriving myself of friends.

To these people, marriage has come to mean a closed, often mechanical dyadic interaction. Respondents emphasized that such dependency on one's mate cannot satisfy the multiple demands of self-development. Gary, divorced three years ago after a ten-year marrige, stated: "It's simplistic to think that one person is always going to fill all my needs and that I'm not going to change and she's not going to change."

Correlative with the lack of self-development is the sense of isolation often felt in an exclusive relationship. This was cited as a second major push. A number of respondents pointed out that marriage, rather than singlehood, paradoxically creates conditions of aloneness they did not want to experience. Marilyn, discussing her marriage, exemplified this problem: "The marriage lasted about five years. . . . I didn't know what I was missing, but I knew I was missing something. I felt a tremendous isolation. . . ."

Loneliness may occur because of an inability to share experiences meaningfully with one's mate. Many respondents described a feeling of disconnectedness and resultant frustration, both psychological and sexual, within the marital relationship which we may identify as a push toward singlehood. Steve noted how the failure to communicate with his wife, while he was involved in graduate school and she with their infant, drew tham apart, creating anger and temporary impotence on his part. Driven to seek relationships with other women, he experienced guilt and further enstrangement from his wife, which subsequently led to his divorce.

Several respondents mentioned the tendency in marriage to associate only with mutually satisfying friends as a push toward the single state. Most often those friends were the husband's, not the wife's. Joan remarked that: "While I was married, I was really upset at how limited the ability to have other friends was." In fact, as Tom suggested, it is the fear of involvement with people that brings about the overinvolvement with a mate: "I find that it is easier for single people to have friends than married people because I think the reason why people get married is to cut down on the amount of friends they have. Marriage is a protective thing. . . ."

Thus, early marriage can constitute a flight from experience. Friendships, which normally make up an important part of one's experience, are not developed. An individual may recognize this pattern, however, and come to desire more interpersonal involvement. Since, for many of our interviewees, marriage has functioned to avoid friendships, loneliness tends to be associated with marriage and accordingly serves as a push away from it.

A final push brought out by a majority of the men and women we interviewed was the idea that marriage restricts opportunities. The dominant view was that marriage is an entrapment, requiring constant accommodation and compromise, which cuts off varieties of experience. In stating his reasons for singlehood, Sven implies these objections to marriage:

> There are conditions under which I would consider getting married. . . . I want freedom of choice, freedom to do what I want instead of being tied to living with just one person and doing the same, mutually satisfying things over and over.

Most respondents concluded that the security and interdependence of marriage inhibits independence, experimentation, and learning. They rejected what they saw as a stalemate, a boring situation.

Men and women offered many positive reasons, many pulls, for remaining single. They spoke of freedom, enjoyment, opportunities to meet people and develop friendships, economic independence, more and better sexual experiences, and personal development. Margaret Adams (1971), cited earlier, suggests three factors that can make being single pleasurable: economic independence, social and psychological autonomy, and a clear intent to remain single by preference. Adams (1974:491) notes that "the unmarried woman has greater freedom to take advantage of the exceptional opportunities for new experiences offered by today's rapidly changing world." Those women who remain unmarried past thirty "are beginning to build up economic independence, an investment in work, and a viable value system that allows them to identify and exploit major sources of personal and social satisfaction in other areas than marriage and family."

Adams' observations are reflected in the responses of the women in our study. Lilith spoke of the abundant opportunities she has available with the attainment of economic self-sufficiency:

> There are so many things I want to do. Now that I've completed school and am making a good living, there is fun to be had. I've started a dance class, learned pottery, and joined a women's group.

While these activities can be pursued by married persons as well, Lilith found that her marriage did not give her the support and encouragement she needed to move toward new activities. The satisfaction of economic independence and the options it presents constitutes a strong pull toward singlehood. Most of the other female respondents corroborated Lilith's experience of finding her time and energies fully taken up in a meaningful life style. The consensus was that marriage or an exclusive relationship would only impinge on the freedom to pursue their personal development.

The pull of psychological autonomy was emphatically brought out by most women respondents, who stated that, theoretically, women can be both married and active in a career and involved in stimulating relationships. But most testified to a feeling of being secondary to the male in an exclusive relationship; they also said that there was a tendency to put his needs ahead of their own. Susan, for example, a psychiatric social worker who had lived with a man for about a year, found herself focusing on her partner's activities and discounting hers. With singlehood came greater self-assurance and motivation. Susan has become involved in several professional activities, particularly in helping to organize a regional conference dealing with health care issues. She reported that she enjoyed her newly felt freedom and that she was developing better professionally.

Alice's experiences underscored the pull of social autonomy in particular. Her three-year monogamous relationship, in which she tried to be all things to her mate—"friend, lover, mother, shrink" —culminated in her feeling like a "victim," isolated from her own needs. Through joining a women's group, her feelings gradually changed. "I started to feel like I really could have other people available to me and . . . it was really possible to get it together with other people." Alice's single life style emphasizes growth through multiple friendships and sexual freedom. Instead of modeling her life on a mate, she began to move outward, enjoying a diversity of human contacts that she was convinced had helped her attain a stronger and clearer sense of selfhood.

Male respondents often cited the pull of more varied experiences. Rather than being bound into the roles of husband, father, and breadwinner, they felt free as singles to try out a plurality of roles, through which they could seek elements of their own identity. Roger mused on some of the options:

> . . . clown, promoter, radical, friend, playboy, priest . . . you name it, the possibilities are there. I'm in a situation to discover my potentials and act on them. It's an exciting process, sometimes frightening, but I like having alternatives to choose from.

Roger's experiences are illustrative of the experiences of many of the other respondents. Roger lived in the same community in Connecticut from the time of birth until college. He went to grammar school a few blocks from his house, and then to the local high school. Pushed toward hard work and achievement, Roger received good grades in high school, played on the football team, and received a substantial scholarship to a college in Massachusetts. During his second year at college, he started dating the young woman who two years later became his wife. She was the first women with whom he had ever had sex. Before they became engaged, in the late fall of his senior year at college, Roger started dating but not having sex with another woman. Once engaged, Roger stopped dating—and talking to—other women. The men's college he attended offered a good academic setting, and intercollegiate sports took up the rest of his time. He married in June after his graduation and then moved to Boston with his new bride to attend Harvard University. While there, he became involved with some local groups trying to open up several store-front schools in Roxbury. After he earned his law degree, Roger returned to Connecticut, where he lived in a garden apartment twenty minutes away from his parents and fifteen minutes away from his wife's parents. A baby girl was born a year later, and Roger was forging a career near Wall Street, commuting three hours each day. As his career advanced, his anger and discomfort grew. On the one hand, he seemed to have the best life possible—an attractive wife, a daughter, and the support of his parents nearby. Yet he worked long hours, easily grew irritable, felt pressured and trapped.

Roger reported feeling trapped by his closely programmed life. He was beginning to meet adults who had travelled and whose work allowed them contact with other groups and new settings—experiences that were missing from his life. At the same time, fights with his wife over financial matters increased; he was embroiled in disagreements with his parents over "appropriate ways" to raise his child. After six years of marriage, and following several nasty fights with his wife, Roger left Connecticut to move in with a work-related colleague who lived in Brooklyn Heights.

Separated for six months at the time of the interview, Roger reported preferring his "more existential" situation as a single.

In many ways, Roger's personal case is typical of many. Although he had the advantges of the middle-class life style passed onto him by his parents, the educational system, and his job, Roger had had very few life experiences. Roger was a culturally and experientially deprived person. Although benefiting from the economic advantages of a middle-class base, his life was essentially devoid of experiences other than culturally prescribed ones. There had been no experiences in his life that would prepare him to deal as a peer with people from backgrounds other than his own. Now, when Roger talks about the new roles he wants to try, he is talking about different ways of relating to people, ways that will put him in contact with different people.

For Roger, the push toward singleness comes out of a desperate need to get some life experience. While he might be criticized by some as a misfit, and while others might wonder what went wrong in a seemingly ideal and blissful marriage, Roger feels he is his own person for the first time in his life. The force and the amount of energy that it took to get him out of his rut comes from the more urgent need to get something going in his life. For him, it was an option for life over desperation. He now enjoys making day-to-day decisions, decisions that are individual instead of joint, decisions that are often spontaneous, based on a changing assessment of his needs. Flexibility in schedule and greater mobility have helped him create a free-flowing, integrated life. He works, studies, travels, and relaxes without the guilt and constraints associated with his former life.

In a more recent contact since the first interview, Roger reported that his wife, since the separation, is also exercising some choices and doing things she had abandoned for wifehood and motherhood. She has just returned to college (having completed two years before marriage) and has decided on a career in nursing. She is feeling better about the decision to separate and feeling better about her life.

The desire for positive experience was also the major motivating force for Cathy, a twenty-six year old teacher with a strong interest in creative writing. She was born in Michigan to a middle-class family, one of three children. Her father was a middle-level executive and her mother a housewife, active in the local P.T.A. Cathy was expected to marry. There was the Junior League, and two years at a nearby junior college. During her last year in high school and throughout the two years in college, Cathy increasingly came to realize that she had the ability to do well in school and that she had some talent for writing. Yet, "in compliance with her parents' expectations," and because "so many of my girl-friends were getting pinned, engaged, and planning weddings," Cathy kept at least one eye out for the "perfect" husband. She met him at the University of Michigan's homecoming game with Ohio State's Buckeyes, when he invited her to the fraternity party following the game. He was an English major and wrote for the literary magazine. They started dating regularly and, at twenty, with the help of parents and relatives and friends, the inevitable wheels of marriage began to churn.

She and Michael would talk of many things, though most had to do with his career and his plans to go to a good graduate school. It wasn't until after their engagement had been announced in the local paper that Cathy allowed herself to show Michael part of the play she had been secretly working on for the past year. When he minimized her efforts as somewhat competent but amateurish, she was disappointed, but she did not yet realize the extent of her hurt. It was not until the plan for the marriage got going and Michael again refused to support Cathy's writing efforts that she began to question her future plans. The long agony ended when Cathy decided to leave Michael, who was headed for Stanford. She also left her parents and moved to Chicago, where, after a frenetic search for a job, she got a day-care center position. She had two women roommates and decided to complete her B.A. She began to feel that there were choices to be made in her life, and that there were many experiences she could have as a single person that were not available to her if she were married. She was afraid, but she was eager for new experiences and the development of friendships with men and women in similar situations. She was trying to make up for the experiences she never had at home as the daughter who was programmed for marriage.

Singlehood can create the conditions through which an individual attains self-respect and confidence which emerged as a major pull, related closely to the psychological autonomy already discussed in relation to women. Although marriage is associated with respon-sibility, many of the single men interviewed believed that being on their own gave them a stronger sense of their capacities by eliminating both pressures and excuses. Jim, who has been married twice and has now lived as a single for five years, noted:

> I am having an experience I never had before. I was always answerable to someone—my family or wife. I never had the experience of being completely self-motivated, of not having to consider someone else's reaction to what I do—their approval or disapproval. Does the job pay enough? It makes me feel potent . . . and very responsible for what I do. Productive. Capable of dealing with life's experiences, and capable even of seeking friendly help when I need it. Whether you are self-realized or not cannot be blamed or credited to someone else.

Both men and women mentioned sexual availability as an important motivation, or pull, for remaining single. They enjoyed the stimulation and variety of an open dating pattern and tended to see their cross-sex relationships in terms of friendship rather than romance. Many respondents testified to the difficulty of achieving a fully open and relaxed accommodation to people of the opposite sex, however. They felt a measure of distance because of their social conditioning, more specifically, they felt limited by the norms of the double standard, by the attitude that sexual intercourse must be condoned by marriage, and by the learning of stereotyped sex roles. Monogamy as a social ideal further perpetuates the distancing of the sexes since it requires guarding against extramarital liaisons. Martin commented:

> I think my upbringing, everybody's upbringing, tended to dichotomize sexual relationships and friendships. With a person of the opposite sex you are either in a sexual relationship or you are not . . . but it is the sexual nature of the relationship that determines the relationship and not the friendly nature of it. That has tended to make enemies out of us.

Still, respondents emphatically chose to work at overcoming their acquired fears and reserves rather than accept the lack of human interaction seemingly imposed by society. Furthermore, many respondents had discovered that the attempt to develop friendly cross-sex relationships was linked to the process of growing closer to members of their own sex.

Others spoke of the increase in cross-sex friendships they had experienced, once they left a sexually exclusive situation, which removed much of the motivation for the possessiveness and jealousy. Steve observed that:

> . . . my wife would be threatened by my having another woman over to talk about a project or work together, whereas being single I can have multiple nonsexual relationships with men and women.

Interviews with Roger and Cathy reveal the complexity of the pushes and pulls experienced by them. For Cathy, the potential of career opportunity, her desire for varied experiences, and the need for change and experimentation with alternatives gained greater salience for her as the more traditional and conventional pushes toward marriage lost salience for her. She never married because she felt that the man to whom she was engaged would not give her the sort of support she needed. Step by step, the attraction of being single grew stronger for her. With the help of new friends facing a similar situation, she changed her priorities. Roger, who had been attracted to marriage because of a number of "pulls," stayed with it for six years. A majority of the people we talked to either tried marriage or a marriage-like situation before they decided that the pushes and pulls toward being single were greater than the pushes and pulls keeping them married or near-married. We do not know if their commitment to being single would be the same had they not had those experiences.

The foregoing comments are not meant to be an indictment of marriage. There are no choices that are intrinsically productive or destructive of personal development; each much be examined. Either the experience of marriage or the experience of singleness may be used in a productive way. It is crucial to ask to what extent the experience supported the development of the two persons.

Our respondents indicate that singlehood provides a situation conducive to human growth and self-fulfillment, and that the framework of marriage is no longer necessary in order to find emotional support, sex, and an active social life. Unencumbered by the constraints of marriage, there was, among the members of our sample, a redirection of social energies and social interaction through which singlehood by choice may be seen as a positive alternative to marriage.

Chapter 7
Sources of Support for Singles

I now have a new group of friends who feel essentially the way I do, and who offer support for my life style, work, my interests and my life in general. But I first had to move away from the suburbs.

What sort of social, emotional, financial, and interpersonal support exists in single people's lives? Is it organized, structured, or spontaneous? Where do singles find their identity?

The questions dealing with friendship were among the most difficult for our interviewees to answer. Most paused for a while, thought, and offered tentative, often halting answers. Several stumbled in their attempts to define friendship, changed their answers, coughed, and seemed otherwise uneasy. The subject itself evoked the discomfort, perhaps because friendship assumes great importance in singles' lives. The themes that emerged from the Older Sample respondents' definitions of friendship included care and support, intensity, reciprocity, acceptance and judgment, honesty, and the sharing of feelings and activities.

CARE AND SUPPORT

Because single persons are generally outside the family institution they look elsewhere for supportive relationships—sometimes in group interaction, but more often in friendship. It took Jim quite a while to define friendship:

> . . . it's hard to pin down . . . definitions are changing. A friend is one who tries; who wants to care, support and help as much as they can [long pause] . . . . Friends forgive shortcomings, without trying to ignore them . . . uh . . . or allow them to try to abuse the relationship. A friend is someone trying to be free of all the familiar parental restrictions.

For Brenda, friendship takes some time to develop—it means "looking at your own behavior, compromising, verbalizing, and really getting to know how somebody feels about something; being able to say you disagree. Respect and caring are very important . . . trying to understand the other person and how they got to be who they are."

INTENSITY

Intensity of friendship is important to some singles. For some of our respondents, intensity was the amount of time spent together; for others it was considered a consequence of the interaction at a particular time, so the same friendship relationship could be more intense at certain times and less so at others.

For Joan, the intensity of the specific interaction is more germane than the amount of time spent together. "Sometimes I can meet someone and have a conversation and just really be super involved in it and the other person is too. And for me that's being a friend at that time." Joan feels that:

> . . . the intensity with which we talk is not a function of any category of time . . . it varies, but the intensity is pretty much a result of how much we communicate . . . feeling really connected and excited about what I'm talking about with the other person.

Intensity is not regarded as a necessary quality of friendship by all informants, however. Mike insisted that friendships do not necessarily have to include being together a great amount of time or in very dramatic situations: "I can be a pretty good friend to someone who I see not more than once every two weeks."

RECIPROCITY

Mike stresses reciprocity in friendship:

> My friends help me be more open and support my saying and acting on what I feel and it's reciprocal. . . . I used to think I could make someone be my friend, but now it's a matter of my being somewhat friendly and their being friendly, and it's cumulative.

Reciprocity is also vital for Tom:

> Sometimes I do things with Bill. He wanted to know who I was and I was interested in knowing something about him, too. He is also someone whom I can help or can help me get things done. The thing to remember is what you did together. . . . A friend is someone I am concerned about as much as he is about me.

ACCEPTANCE AND JUDGMENT

Several persons felt that a friend is one who accepts you, but who also has the right or responsibility to be helpfully critical. Marilyn replied that for her a friend is:

> . . . someone who accepts you . . . I was going to say who doesn't judge you, but I don't think that's true. . . . A friend really suits you, realizes your shortcomings, and still finds you valuable as a person. It is friendly to mention shortcomings. I may not like it, but I can accept it.

HONESTY

Honesty was also important to many:

> . . . somebody you could be as honest with as you want to be . . . you know . . . better still, where you want to be as honest, where you don't want to get into faking it . . . where just being together can be fun.

SHARING OF FEELINGS AND ACTIVITIES

A number of people stress the sharing of various experiences, activities, and feelings as an important part of friendship. "A friend is someone you can have fun with—share the good times and the bad times—the dreams, your hopes."

Barbara talked about changes in her definition of friendship:

> It has shifted a lot. [pause] I used to think of a friend as someone who would be very interested in problems and stick by you, true blue. . . . I think that's unrealistic now. . . . I think a friend is somebody to do things with.

For Susan, friends are people "I can rely on . . . If I need them they'll be there. People I can have a good time with and share similar values with and can relate to on that basis."

For David, a sense of feeling at ease is important.

> With a friend, I'll feel at ease and don't have to put on my best face. I'll feel comfortable with them. . . . I can say what's on my mind and they'll listen and won't be scared. . . . They will be comfortable with me.

For some, like Barbara, friendship entails an effort and energy which people may not want to invest at a particular time.

> It takes a lot of time and work, and I am in a pretty selfish mood right now. I don't feel I can spend that time concentrating on somebody else's head. . . .

Generally, it seems that respondents expressed rather modest expectations of friendship. They did not, as a group, define it as a relationship of undying loyalty and unqualified acceptance. They were tolerant of the notion that friends may come and go. The enduringness of the friendship did not seem to be a primary issue. Rather, it was the appropriateness and commonality of the relationship in the moment that was most important.

FRIENDS AND FRIENDSHIPS

We asked our respondents whether it was easier for them to have same- or opposite-sex friendships. Forty-nine per cent of Sample A said it was easier for them to have the same-sex friends. For twenty-eight per cent, it made no difference, and for nineteen per cent opposite-sex friends were easier to have. (Four per cent did not respond.) The same pattern held for Sample B people. One-half said same-sex friendships were easier and about one-fifth found opposite-sex friends easier to have. Thirty per cent reported that sex made no difference. Membership in various kinds of men's and women's groups has eased the development of same-sex friendships, a more recent experience for most of our respondents.

To the extent that dating patterns tend to set limits on the degree of openness and honesty between men and women, limits are also placed on friendships between the sexes. Most first cross-sex friendships seem to develop in the context of romance. Cross-sex relations are often nonequalitarian, less reciprocal, of shorter duration, and less honest. Many cross-sex relations reported by our sample met only some of the criteria of friendship as defined by the respondents themselves.

For many, support came both from past opposite-sex primary partners and same-sex friends. Some felt that among their best friends was a man or a woman they had once lived with or to whom they had been married. Some of these relationships were long standing.

Marilyn, who has been married twice, voices the experiences of some. In both marriages, her husband was also her best friend, but particularly in her first marriage.

> It was my husband and I against the world. In my second marriage, my husband was also my best friend, but my female friends became important to me and they've continued to be so. . . . There are a few things I can't say to my better female friends, but there's a slew of things I would never say to a man. I think certain honesties, if you're feeling vulnerable, you can't admit or if you're feeling hurt they're hard to admit. I have an image of having to feel very strong . . . screaming I don't care, while deep down I really care."

Ellen shares these feelings. Her first boyfriend, with whom she lived, is still one of the people who knows her best.

> When we lived together, he was the best friend I had, and we're still in touch as friends even though he's married. But he was not what a girl-friend was—girlfriends fulfilled emotional needs while men have fulfilled societal needs. I needed to have a boyfriend, and I felt involved with men, but when it came to really sharing things, unhappiness, or laying open my soul, I would go to a girlfriend.

The relationship between sex and friendship is complex. Fifty-four per cent of Sample A respondents felt that having sexual relations did not support friendship. Twenty-three per cent felt the opposite, and another twenty-three per cent were not sure whether sexual relations supported or hindered friendship.

The responses of Sample B members were fairly evenly divided. For some, sex hinders the development of cross-sex friendships. Mike reported that:

> . . . it's harder to be a friend with a female because I get confused with the old idea of sex coming in it. . . . Sex interferes with friendship. This doesn't happen with men . . . the impediment of sex isn't there. I get intimidated and scared around sex.

Jim, who had been married and who had later lived in a monogamous relationship with a second woman, feels that:

> . . . sex is a weapon . . . it's a way of asserting power. For some men it's a way of asserting their masculinity, and for some women it's a way of asserting their submissiveness. They have something we want them to surrender.

A number of persons felt sexual tension in cross-sex friendships where there was no sex. Dan reported:

> It often felt unreal to me, like there was something missing, and yet I feared that sexual involvement might have destroyed a developing friendship. At that time a friendship with a woman was more important for me than just some more sex.

Lynda also feels these difficulties. She had learned the "social games" early in her dating career: "To manipulate boys. They just want to have sex with you and don't really care anyway . . . they are out to seduce you and I'm out-seducing them."

For Brenda, two men she dates on a regular basis provide important support. She feels that both know her well:

> . . . they know things about me and can help me in situations. They know basically who I am, in varying degrees, both of them, and can

see a problem that I might be having even without my saying it, and be able to help me.

When asked how her friendships with women differ, Brenda had a hard time pinpointing the difference:

> I feel often that I want to please men psychologically and sexually; my feeling unequal with men is a handicap. It's a problem I want to work on. . . . With women, I am not so concerned about pleasing them.

Other respondents did not feel that sex gets in the way, but that it is a nice and pleasurable way to communicate. Joan says that she likes sex and that it helps intimacy: "You can become intimate through conversation, through touching, holding. Having sex, the closeness increases." For Paul, too, sex has helped to develop intimacy and bring pleasure: "It can be a beautiful experience to share."

Why should there be a difference in expectations between the same-sex and opposite-sex friends? The few empirical studies that exist suggest that the differences start at an early age. Douvan and Adelson (1966) reported that male–male friendships in adolescence are less intimate than female–female friendships. In Booth's 1972 study of adults in two urban communities, he noted that, while males have more friends than females, men's friendships are described as less close and less spontaneous. Female friendships are affectionately richer. Adams in another study (1968) reported less intimacy, on the average, between men than between women friends.

Booth (1972) also reported that men with a "high need for affiliation and affect" were rated by other men as having *negative* qualities. Sociability and communication about matters peripheral to the self are supported; but intimacy—the sharing of feelings and thoughts central to oneself—in those relationships is less acceptable for men than for women in our society.

Joseph Pleck (1975) reports that changes in the importance of male institutions and the shift in emphasis from male friendships to earlier heterosexual experiences has shortened adolescence, eliminating the time in which social ties and experiences with other males are explored. Adolescent males asserting their independence from family ties is now a phenomenon that occurs in the context of a relationship with girlfriends rather than with another male. What are the results of this for later male–female relationships? Pleck suggests that there is greater distrust, even outright hatred, of women for blocking earlier needs for male affiliation and friendships. Some of those blocked needs surface later through men's desires for same-sex friendships in their twenties and thirties. The emergence of men's groups represents such structures for male friendships and provides a setting within which men can develop more skills for handling intimate relationships with other men. There they can deal with competitiveness, achievement drives, and with the fear of homosexuality, all of which get in the way of male friendships.

How do friendships develop? How active a role do people take in their development? How easy or difficult is it to develop friendships? What sort of boundaries do people set on friendships? Questions such as these sought to elicit the dynamics of friendship formation; the answers revealed a number of interesting responses. While few respondents said they had an easy time developing friendships, some took a much more active role in seeking friends than did others. Some respondents felt comfortable initiating and pursuing friendships; others played a more passive role. These differences cut across sex and age lines.

In her earlier experiences of friendship with men, Joan felt she had to follow a certain time schedule.

You couldn't do *this* before *that,* and it had to be sort of ritualistic. And you had to wait a certain amount of time before you could *do X* and another certain amount of time before you could *do Y* and so on. Time determined how friendship should proceed, even introducing someone to your friends. I see boundaries to some extent, more or less defined by an awareness of where the other person is at, what they can and cannot do. So the boundaries and limits are about them and also about me.

Barry recalls that "I used to think I could manipulate people into being my friends. I realize now I can't. Friendship is cumulative, a bit at a time." Barry goes on to talk about some difficulties he has around friendship; particularly, "my unwillingness to open myself to others." He had always felt that "openness is inconsistent with your well-being. . . . It's really important to guard yourself. Now I'm trying to unlearn that."

Reciprocity and trust take some time to develop. Brenda talked about how:

> There's one woman that when we get together I have a good time, but we always say we should see each other more often, but for some reason we don't. We feel good when we're together, but there may be gaps in between, and gaps bother me.

Friendship, clearly, played an important part in the lives of the Sample B single people we interviewed. They did not in any sense seem to conform to the old stereotype of lonely singles. Other forms of support were also available. A variety of more or less structured organizations provided settings that allowed singles to talk about themselves. Women's groups, for example, were reported by several women to be the first step they made toward getting out of marriage.

Another set of questions related to membership in various groups and organizations: from consciousness-raising groups, men's and women's activity-friendship groups, and rap groups for singles, to adult courses, to therapy groups, to group living, or to urban communes. Some of these groups, like the singles rap groups, are organized directly for singles. Others are simply group situations organized for a variety of purposes in which singles may find an audience for their experiences and a place to meet and hang out.

WOMEN'S GROUPS AND MEN'S GROUPS

For Maureen, her women's group provided much needed support for her movement away from an exclusive relationship with a man:

I started to feel like I could really have other people available to me, and I really could get needs met through other people. . . . About five or six months ago it crystallized in my head that I needed to see other men as well as women, and it was a very difficult thing for me to work out.

For Barbara, the women in her group:

. . . helped me to realize that you don't need a man to help you start doing things. There's no reason I have to feel life is not complete without a man . . . my women friends are helping me cope.

Several of our male respondents belonged to a men's group for single or both single and married men. Some of these groups were identified as consciousness-raising groups, and some were formed for friendship or for activities, but the emphasis in the groups is on open sharing of experiences and feelings. At times a group planned a specific activity such as a picnic, a camping weekend, or a softball game, which allowed members to know each other better through shared experiences.

Jan felt that the men's group could provide support for his single status:

We talk about all kinds of things—women, work, and sometimes about marriage and kids. About four of the guys were married and are fathers, and I just don't feel that I want to go through the hassles they did.

Barry related the painful story of his marital separation and the kind of support his male friends provided:

I started crying at one of the meetings, and the guys were just there. . . . I was afraid that they would laugh and call me a fool, but Jim started talking about the pain he felt years earlier around his separation, and I stopped feeling alone.

What Barry learned was that "as we began to talk about our problems and feelings we began to realize that individuals trying to solve problems often resulted in loneliness and frustration. . . .

It was important to find out that others faced the same problems I had."

Some of our respondents had participated in one or more specialized groups which brought them together with other singles in rap and discussion groups, study groups, and groups centering around the arts. At this writing, a number of churches in metropolitan areas across the country sponsor such evenings for singles. The participants are randomly assigned to one of fifteen or twenty groups with about twelve to fourteen persons in each group. Some of the leaders are formally trained in the social sciences; others are not. Leaders introduce the topic for the evening, and each group separately discusses the same topic. These include such questions as: "How have you changed in the last several years?" "Why are you single?" "What does it take to have a healthy relationship?" One night a week might be scheduled for single parents, and another night for gay and bisexual singles who discuss their particular experiences and problems. Discussion leaders encourage full participation, guide the discussion, and summarize at the end of the two hour meeting. In one Unitarian church in New York City, the 400-person capacity is filled quickly, and with the $3.00 or $4.00 per person admission fee, the singles group provides a good source of revenue for the church.

It is difficult to say what proportion of men and women attending a singles rap group on any evening has been there before; but according to the estimates of several group leaders, over one-half of the participants return at least once and some are in attendance almost every week. The groups provide a relatively friendly, low-keyed setting in which singles can talk to each other. For the group leaders, it provides even more of a supportive setting, since they meet on a weekly basis by themselves to share their group experiences, to evaluate various discussion strategies, to assess the effectiveness of various topics, and, to some extent, to talk about their own lives.

The last few years have also witnessed the beginning of adult education course offerings for singles. Among universities offering courses in the singles experience are The New School for Social Research, Lehman College, Hunter College and the Women's

Center in New York City, and The University of Southern California. Three useful source books for singles appeared recently: *The Challenge of Being Single* by Marie Edwards and Eleanor Hoover, the *Survival Guide for the Suddenly Single* by Barbara Berson and Ben Bova, and *Coping: A Survival Manual for Women Alone* by Martha Yates. Psychologist Margaret Adams is completing a book on single women; and sociologist Robert Staples is gathering data for a book on single blacks. A group called All Together, Inc. in Chicago, Illinois purports to exist to represent all singles and to give them a chance to be heard.

All of these specialized groups, organizations, and adult education courses offer singles an opportunity to meet each other in helpful settings. The goals of all these activities are to help single men and women deal with problems, discuss issues, learn about themselves and others, and have fun with each other. In this way they provide support settings for singles.

SINGLES' LIVING SITUATIONS

We asked our respondents about their current living situations. Some of them lived alone, while others lived with roommates. Some live in urban communal groups, sharing large apartments and even buildings—living arrangements which provide readily available support for a single life style founded on the development of friendships.

For Gary, who had been married for ten years, the support came from "the three guys I share an apartment with, and with whom I share similar attitudes about life." Like-minded peers are essential for support. For Jim, quoted at the opening of this chapter, the support came from seeking out and being sought by others with similar attitudes and orientations.

Communes constitute an important form of social support for some single people. Preliminary evidence from an extensive study of urban communes by Benjamin Zablocki suggests that most of the experiences reported by our respondents were also recorded by his much larger sample of men and women living in six urban cities of the United States: Los Angeles, Minneapolis, Houston, Atlanta, Boston, and New York. The *Urban Communes Project* includes almost 700 men and women, living in various communes, including religious, political, craft, music, art, and therapeutically-oriented communes. Some of the communes were guided by a specific ideology, while others were merely places people chose to share because it was economically feasible. Some of the communes are organized and have regular meetings as frequently as once a day; others meet only when there are financial matters needing attention. Some of the communes have children, but most do not. Most of the communards are single, while some are married and others are involved in sexually exclusive relationships. All of the communes studied included both men and women.

Why do people join communes? The number and variety of reasons represent a broad spectrum of motivation. Some join for primarily economic reasons: It is cheaper to live with others than to live alone. For others, communes offer greater order and regularity than did their earlier, more chaotic lives. For most, it is a need for support and for friendships among people who care in a world they see as mostly non-caring. For some it is a way to leave home, to get away from parents, and to live in a more stimulating and interesting environment. For almost all, it represents some sort of break with the past and a search for a viable alternative to things they had tried but did not like. It is also exploratory for many—a way of trying out a new life style merely for the sake of new experience. For some, it is a way to live with a lover; for others, it represents a way to live in the single state in the company of others. It is a search for like-minded people. For some, it is primarily a search for companionship; for others, it is a search for community.

Preliminary results from the *Urban Communes Project* suggested the kinds of support members of communes feel they receive. One series of questions asked whether communal living made it easier or harder to do a series of activities. Depending on the activity, between seventy and eighty-two per cent felt it was *easier* in communal living to meet new people; to solve emotional problems; to meet financial emergencies; to be the kind of person you want to be; to relate to people actively, openly, and spontaneously; to find out who you are; to be cared for when you are physically ill; to find out what you want in life—and to be single.

Table IX
Activities Made Easier by Communal Living

Activity	Percentage (N = 478)
To be single	70%
To find out what you want in life	70%
To be the kind of person you want to be	72%
To meet financial emergencies	72%
To find out who you are	74%
To meet new people	77%
To relate to people openly and spontaneously	80%
To solve emotional problems	81%
To be cared for when physically ill	82%

Source: Benjamin Zablocki, *Urban Communes Project,* Columbia University, 1975, unpublished data.

Despite the variation in the kinds of communes that comprised the sixty communes in the sample, there is fairly high uniformity regarding the reported advantages of communal living.

The range of motivations reveals a great heterogeneity. For some, the process of joining a commune was a hard one; others joined friends who were already there. Some groups had a relatively easy time finding a place to live. For example, preliminary reports of data suggest that it was easier for communes in Houston, Los Angeles, and Boston to find housing than it was for people in Minneapolis and Atlanta. The average stay in a commune is about two years. Some are satisfied with their communal experience and merely move to another commune in a new town or a new state. Some move from one type of commune to another in the same town. Some try to change the structure of their current commune, and, unable to do so to their satisfaction, move to another commune more to their liking. Some of the communards move to marry—often to persons they met while living in the commune. Some just drop out of the commune to return to an earlier life style.

A significant proportion of the men and women interviewed by the staff of the *Urban Communes Project* were steadily employed and led very "normal" lives outside of their communal living experiences. They were not "freaks" or "way-out people," but men and women who were pursuing undergraduate and graduate education, or careers, and who had chosen living arrangements which offered friendly, supportive environments.

David Bradford and Simon Klevansky (1975) reported on a study of fifteen communes in the San Francisco area which they termed "middle-class communes." The number of persons living in the communes ranged from five to fourteen, with the average about eight per household. In many ways, their sample was very similar to "any urban counterculture commune." Respondents were asked to rate the importance to them of reasons for living communally. The five reasons most often cited were:

1. Interpersonal contact and relationship to others.
2. Sense of community—belonging to a larger group.
3. Chance for personal growth.
4. Better setting for children to grow and develop.
5. Chance for deep, intimate relationships.

As with Zablocki's study, a majority of the respondents were single. They included men and women who were lawyers, school teachers, engineers, therapists, computer programmers, professors, ministers, managers, and salesmen. Most joined urban communes not so much out of economic need as because they were in search of a community. The authors suggest that urban middle-class communes will increase in frequency in the future.

For most of the single men and women in our sample who did not live alone, shared living arrangements were a vital source of support. The support was evident in a number of ways. The presence of roommates meant the presence of other people to share experiences with, to have a drink with, to talk to, to catch up on the day's experiences, or just to say hello to. It proved to be an effective way of dealing with previously felt isolation and loneliness. It was also easier to meet new people through one's roommates than through other means. Phil noted:

There is always someone around to talk to when I want to take a break from work, or just to throw the frisbee. It is different from my college dorm. We all want to be here, and we're becoming good friends. We're getting the apartment into shape, making it a comfortable place to live.

CONCLUSION

The basis on which a successful single life style rests is economic independence, which, in turn, promotes a sense of dignity and self-esteem. While the importance of self-sustaining work applies to both sexes, it was dramatically evident in the cases of the women interviewed, since they had consciously rejected the traditional female role of dependence on a husband's income and status. Those who had experienced identification with a mate's career, and had subsequently attained social status through their own careers, stressed an increase in pride and a stronger sense of selfhood. They cited advances in their career development, greater interest in work, and a gradual investment in a professional identity. As yet, women still have to struggle for jobs, and they make an average of sixty per cent of male salaries in equivalent full-time jobs; but there is a mood of hopefulness as the doors are opened (Ehrlich, et al., 1975). The viability of singlehood for women is contingent on access to economic opportunities (Adams, 1974).

The single men interviewed mentioned a heightened sense of choice about their work because they did not have to be as security-conscious as males with families. They were able to make professional commitments based on interest and mobility; they enjoyed the knowledge that they could explore other fields, if they wished, with relatively little risk. Both sexes, of course, derived satisfaction from having the freedom to choose how to spend their money, by not being tied down to joint financial decisions.

Virtually all the persons interviewed in the Older Sample spoke of having more friends as one of the advantages of being single. A common complaint about an exclusive relationship is the tendency to limit oneself to mutual friends and having others relate to one as part of a couple rather than as an individual. Interviewees mistrusted the intensity of an exclusive relationship, which they found restricting to each partner. As singles, they felt free to explore particular interests that had been neglected in a marriage-like situation unless their mate happened to share the same interest.

Both men and women perceived more opportunities in their lives as singles, which they were attempting to explore. They spoke of taking classes, dating widely, learning music or a sport, traveling, trying new roles they had been afraid to try before. A number had made critical changes in jobs or schooling made possible by their single status. In one way or another, then, most persons testified to an awareness of personal growth.

These men and women had achieved a viable single life style because of the presence of certain factors. Because they were middle-class and well-educated, they had stable incomes to provide the basis for their independence. Their interpersonal relations had generated social support structures. The presence of other persons and groups served the critical functions of providing a community of peers and validating the choice to stay single. The structures included membership in men's and women's groups, from consciousness-raising to primarily social groups, to group living. Living with other singles provided a key source of emotional support for many people we spoke to, as well as providing the advantage of economic cooperation.

Despite the resources provided by such peer groups, the singles we spoke to nonetheless testified to problems. They are coping with the pressures of a pro-marriage environment—which confronts all singles. Single people described feeling uncomfortable or defensive in society-at-large—with their work associates, for instance, and in couple-dominated social situations. Their families often applied pressure to get married, implying that the single adults were not living up to their responsibilities, or fearing that eventually they would find themselves all alone in the world.

Indeed, *the fear of loneliness is the major problem single people confront.* The fear that one's associates will sooner or later go their separate ways leaving a single person without close ties, or the attitude that one's family will provide support while friends could prove fickle or undependable in a crisis, are used as arguments against remaining single—often, in fact, by singles themselves in moments of doubt. Until recently, some women have found it difficult to lead an active social life without mates, and in many areas of the country this is still true. Isolation and loneliness are associated with the stereotypes of the unmarried woman more than with the traditional image of the bachelor, since women have been expected to find their identity in terms of their families. Single parents, too, often feel overwhelmed by the demands of children and are cut off from the support of other adults, the consequences of which tends to be a desperate search for a new mate instead of cooperative arrangements with other single parents.

We may conclude, then, that a viable single life style depends upon social acceptance and upon ways people can interact meaningfully. Singles need to achieve a sense of relatedness with others over a period of time, to develop patterns of interdependence, and to become mentally and emotionally engaged with fellow beings.

Chapter 8
The Future of Singles in America

Sociologists and philosophers of social science complain, and legitimately so, that there is no one paradigm to guide our research. A paradigm is a taken-for-granted way of looking at the world. It may start as a theory, such as the Copernican theory that the sun, rather than the Earth, is the center of the solar system, or Einstein's theory of relativity. Once accepted, a paradigm becomes integrated into our perceived reality (Kuhn, 1962). But, as Arlene Skolnick notes, "A paradigm also acts like a blinder. A scientist, for example, when immersed in a particular paradigm, will reject or misperceive facts that cannot be fitted into the paradigm" (1973:27).

A paradigm tells us what to observe and what is trivial; it tells us what kinds of information are central to our project and what to push to the background. It gives us focus. Depending upon the focus we choose, we can look at a university as a set of build-

ings in an area of land; we can see the university as a place where
students and faculty gather for the pursuit of knowledge; or we can
look at it as a place to have a good time and meet a potential
mate. We can see a university as a major socialization agency, sort-
ing people out according to social class and instructing them in
appropriate behavior. We can also see a university acting as a
feeding agency for corporations and industry, or as an institution
that keeps young adults out of the labor market for four additional
years.

The model we choose gives us a set of glasses through which
to see the subject—its present, past, and future. It lets us see
certain things and shut out others. It can create the future because
it partly controls it. By defining the categories and the words
through which we perceive the future, the paradigm or model
molds the future in those terms. The model is not only a statement
of what is, but, more important, it is a statement of what is con-
ceivable and desirable. It is impossible to accomplish what is totally
unimaginable. People act on the basis of the possible, of the con-
ceivable. Therefore, the future does not exist outside of the present,
but in relation to and as a reflection of what can be conceived
in the present—which is why the familiar is often transformed into
a sense of the inevitable.

Noam Chomsky (1968:21) notes that ". . . one difficulty in the
psychological sciences lies in the familiarity of the phenomena with
which they deal. A certain intellectual effort is required to see
how such phenomena can pose serious problems or call for in-
tricate explanatory theories. One is inclined to take them for
granted as necessary or somehow 'natural'."

A discussion of models is relevant in any evaluation of trends.
It helps to explain why change is difficult, and why predicting
change is like trying to pick up one foot while the other foot is
holding it down. It also encourages a closer look at trends to see
if they are in the direction of real change.

Essentially, marriage is still the preferred model for living in our
society. It is the frame of reference. But there has been expanded
experimentation among adults seeking other life styles in the past
decades, and there is a growing question as to whether or not the

family will continue to function as the setting for personality development and emotional need satisfaction. Many argue that the family has never done a very good job of either. Still, just as the concept of singlehood has meaning only relative to the concept of marriage, so alternative life styles only have meaning relative to the nuclear family.

The idea of change is no less frightening and awesome for social scientists than for the rest of the population. At the base of the difficulty is the fact that marriage and family are crucially linked to all other institutions of society.

SINGLEHOOD vs. THE STATUS QUO

Try to imagine what our society might be like if seventy-five per cent of the population were single instead of married. When you begin to fantasize the changes that would be wrought, you see the reason behind the fear of change.

What, for instance, would happen to architecture, to the design of space? Would there be a demand for more open space for broader interactions among residents? How would homes, apartments, and summer homes be designed to suit the needs of single persons? Would there be more group and communal dwellings? Would space be utilized to accommodate groups that might expand and contract more quickly than do traditional families?

How would the distribution of population change? What would become of bedroom communities, of the suburbs? Would single people live there, or would there be a shift back to the cities? Where would new communities of single persons develop? And how would they affect the need for mass transportation, for new roads? How would they affect commuting patterns or automobile-buying habits?

How would advertising change? How would consumption patterns change? How would schools change? And what would happen to those industries that cater specifically to the family or to the marriage market?

Would consumption change radically? Of course it would. Either there would be an upsurge in individual products for individual consumers—or more products would be shared among single adults. Either there would be a decline in conspicuous consumption, with less pressure to keep up with the Jones family (since the Jones family would be virtually non-existent), or there would be a similar pressure to keep up with a myriad of single Joneses.

Take the fantasy further. How would politicians maintain an image of honesty, integrity, stability, and moral character without the backing of a family? What would happen to politics and to big business without the traditional transference of power from one generation to the next? As of 1975, 150 of the largest 500 corporations in the United States were still controlled by families (Anderson, 1975). It is by keeping the family intact, and by keeping watch over marital arrangements, that powerful families tend to keep control over their investments. For a full discussion of power transmission in powerful families, read William Domhoff's *Who Rules America?* (1967) and *The Higher Circles* (1970).

Another area that could experience radical change is employment. It is said that the economic stability of our society rests on "full" employment; but "full" employment, even in the best of times, excludes four to five per cent of the working population who are unemployed—and it also excludes married women with children, who are not included in the "working population." Currently, the unemployment rate is increasing to between eight and nine per cent of the population; and it is as high as thirty-five to forty per cent in certain segments of the population, such as among young black men. If the majority of the population were single, the unemployment problem might reach catastrophic proportions. We would either have to have *real* full employment or about a quarter of the population would require public assistance. Without marriage, some women could no longer rely on their husband's income, just as some husbands could no longer rely on wives' income or on their performance of housekeeping chores.

The fact is that the stability of our economy relies on partial employment, which could be one reason that increasing singlehood is regarded as a threat to the status quo.

POSSIBLE TRENDS

National studies are revealing a pattern of discontent with traditional marriage. Longitudinal studies systematically report that disenchantment, disengagement, and corrosion mark the developmental course of marriage. Arlene Skolnick (1973:218) finds "a decline over time in the following areas: companionship, demonstration of affection, including both kissing and intercourse, common interests, common beliefs and values, beliefs in the permanence of marriage, and marital adjustment." Feelings of loneliness are often increased in the very relationships that are supposed to be a refuge from it. There is an increasing realization on the part of counselors, psychologists, and sociologists that, contrary to conventional wisdom, marital stability does not necessarily indicate marital satisfaction.

Active experimentation with alternatives to the nuclear family underscores the discontent with marriage as a norm; and there has been a growth in the number and the type of nontraditional family forms in the late 1960s into the 1970s, with open marriage, group or multilateral marriage, communal family living, cohabiting couples, one-parent families, partner-swapping, and the like. Singlehood represents one of the most significant of the alternatives in terms of the numbers of people who have chosen it as an alternative.

There has been a delay in marriage among young men and women in recent years (See Chapter 2.) Paul Glick (1975:4) identifies several reasons for this trend: an increase in the number of women going to college, an "excess of young women of the ages when marriage rates are highest," an increase in the number of women now employed and the strength and ideological support of the women's movement.

As of this writing, it is too early to know whether or not the single alternative is temporary or permanent, or even whether or not it is an emerging life-long status for a substantial number of persons.

Just as youth has become a new stage in the life cycle in the United States (Keniston, 1971), Matthew Greenwald and Carl Danziger (1975:9) have suggested that transadulthood, yet another stage, is emerging in response to social change. A period from about age eighteen into the late twenties or early thirties, trans-adulthood "is a period of experimenting with different life styles, of searching for career orientation and testing educational goals. . . . The desire to keep options open, to be constantly flexible and prepared for change is characteristic of the transadult." (1975:9).

Daniel Levinson identifies the years from the early twenties to about twenty-seven through twenty-nine as the period of "getting into the adult world," where the focus of one's life shifts from the "family of origin to a new home base in an effort to form an adult life of one's own." (1974:246). It is a time of "exploration and initial choice . . . exploratory searching, provisional choices." (1974:247). It is a time of assessing the correctness of initial choices and of increasing commitment to choices. Between the ages of twenty-eight and thirty-two, people enter a *transitional period* marked by either a deeper commitment to an occupation and a stable life structure or a rejection of the initial occupational choice as "too constricting, a violation or a betrayal of an early dream." (1974:248) Earlier marriage may also be rejected. The age thirty transition may involve considerable turmoil, confusion and struggle with society, with family, and with oneself.

The transitional period is followed by the *settling down period,* which involves "order, stability, security, control . . . building a nest" and "making it: planning, striving, moving onward and up-ward, ambition." Settling down involves marriage and family; but the two aspects ("building a nest" and "making it") are separable (1974:249). In fact, according to Margaret Adams (1974), by age thirty most "women who are not married are beginning to build up economic independence, and investment in work, and a viable system that allows them to identify and exploit major sources of personal and social satisfaction in other areas than marriage and family." Perhaps, for singles, Levinson's model needs revision. One can "make it" and be an adult and yet, at the same time, he or she can be single. Marriage need not be a pre-requisite for adulthood. In this book, we've suggested that complex historical, economic, social, and personal reasons are accounting for the increase in the number of single men and women; and that these factors may be creating a social situation as well as a social status that will be viable for a greater number of men and women. As singlehood gains acceptance and wider normative support, adulthood will no longer be linked with marriage and parenthood.

Unlike other stages of the life cycle, one can return to a single status. As Glick (1975) suggests, some may find singleness a more attractive experience than marriage, and what began as a delay in marriage may extend into permanent singleness over one's lifetime.

A 1974 national survey asked young men and women between the ages of fourteen and twenty-five what life styles they viewed as most appealing. Among the young men, twenty-four per cent chose the single life as the most appealing of the alternatives, while among the young women, seventeen per cent chose that life style. Asked what they expect to be fifteen years hence, nine per cent of the men and five per cent of the women expect to be "a single person with a good job, living well in an apartment in a major city" (Institute of Life Insurance, 1974).

The answers suggest that those who plan to remain single after graduating from school regard it as a transitional stage, not as a permanent status. Susan Jacoby (1974) has suggested that single women, even those making substantial salaries, are less likely to make financial investments which would help provide them with future financial security. Jacoby's suggestion, in turn, provides further evidence that, at least among young women, the single state is seen as a transition.

Still, as discussed in Chapter 7, what appears to account for much of the difference among our respondents in their commitment to being single is the support they receive for that decision. Perhaps if more support were available, there would be fewer people who regard marriage and the nuclear family as the major model for their adult life style.

POSITIVE IDEOLOGY

While there is clearly more support now than there was a generation ago for those who continue to defer marriage, there is little support for those who choose to remain single for long periods of time or for those who choose to remain single into their thirties and beyond.

Women and men who remain single by choice may still be subject to self-doubt and to considerable economic and social discrimination. Like all minority groups, they have a need for an ideology which would enable them to articulate and support their alternative life style.

A positive ideology might facilitate the emergence of single-hood as a social movement, one that would certainly overlap with other liberation movements. Lewis Killian (1973) identifies three elements of a social movement: It begins in response to sources of discontent, has a set of goals, and subsequently evolves a program to implement the goals. As evidenced by our respondents' comments, many people choose to be single in part because they are pushed by the restrictions of marriage. Their goals are variously cited as self-development, change, interaction, freedom of choice, and more varied opportunities. Their program, tentative so far, centers on the development of social and personal support structures, and, additionally, on the elimination of social biases and discrimination.

The heterogenity of the singles population makes the development of a cohesive ideology, with its body of shared meaning, difficult; yet it is a group that comprises a rather large segment of our society which has not received much attention. Singles are a minority in the United States, and, as such, they are subject to discrimination experienced by other minority groups in our society. It would be frivolous and misleading to suggest that singles are a heavily oppressed minority; but they are, nevertheless, a minority, and are generally treated as such. Furthermore, their internal dynamics can be understood in terms of minority group dynamics. With awareness, consciousness-raising, and a sense of common experience can come legitimacy, purpose, goals, and action.

Singles differ from other minority groups in one major aspect: They can usually change their status and gain approval from society. But is marriage worth the approval gained? To many who have tried marriage, it is not.

The greatest need single people feel in their departure from the traditional family structure is for substitute networks of human relationships that provide the basic satisfactions of intimacy, sharing, and continuity. This theme emerged in our interviews through the emphasis respondents placed on their friendships and interpersonal (bonding) activities.[1] Support from like-minded people appeared to be an essential psychological condition for choosing to be single. Although individuals may be driven into singlehood through a negative reaction to marriage, they cannot sustain the state for long without support from people who care about them. Our respondents reported that the context of their supportive relationships differed from the family environment in being more open and more subject to change as well as being based on a sense of choice and free exchange. While the respondents emphasized the importance of variety and change, they were also virtually unanimous in upholding the value of close, caring friendships that lasted over a period of time.

More formal structures are emerging to provide intimacy and continuity among single adults—in forms that range from rap groups to group living.

As Caroline Bird has written (1972:348), the satisfaction of caring and daily involvement are being provided by a variety of groups in ways that are frequently more successful than traditional marriage:

> Not the least of these is the frankly experimental and informal character of the group which encourages exploration of the psyche of the other and dispenses with sanctions that shrivel mutuality.

The collective portrait that emerges is one of single persons who are trying to forge a meaningful life in a society that, though changing, continues to uphold marriage and the family as the model for interpersonal bonding. While the experience of being single is beset by problems and pressures created in part by re-

---

[1]For further analysis and examples of interpersonal bonding, see James Ramey, *Intimate Friendships* (Englewood Cliffs, New Jersey: Prentice-Hall, Inc., 1976.)

strictive social attitudes, singlehood as an alternative life style is in the process of cultural emergence.

A FURTHER WORD

The author hopes that this book and the several others cited will signal the beginning of serious research into the experiences of single men and women. There is a need for both further data and theory on the lives and the future of the 47 million Americans who are single.

Since the research on singles is just beginning, there are currently more questions to be asked than there are available answers: When and why are decisions made to remain single or to marry, to cohabit or to separate? Who chooses singlehood? Who is pushed into marriage—and who is pushed into singlehood as a reaction against marriage? What support structures will continue to emerge for those who choose to remain single?

The answers will emerge only with further research.

APPENDIX

Table X
Marital Status of the Population (Age 18 and Over) by
Sex and Age, 1975

Marital Status	Total Population (18 and Over)	Percentage of Total Population	18 & 19	20 to 24	25 to 29
Men					
Single	14,098,000	21.0%	93.1%	59.9%	22.3%
Separated	1,250,000	1.8%	--	1.1%	2.7%
Divorced	2,545,000	3.8%	--	1.4%	4.2%
Widowed	1,817,000	2.7%	--	0.1%	0.1%
Married	47,525,000	70.7%	6.4%	36.7%	69.8%
TOTAL	67,235,000	100%			
Women					
Single	11,007,000	14.7%	77.7%	40.3%	13.6%
Separated	2,305,000	3.1%	0.9%	3.6%	4.5%
Divorced	3,978,000	5.3%	0.6%	3.5%	6.5%
Widowed	10,104,000	13.5%	0.1%	0.3%	0.5%
Married	47,366,000	63.4%	19.6%	51.0%	74.0%
TOTAL	74,760,000	100%			

Table X (*cont.*)

30 to 34	35 to 39	40 to 44	45 to 54	55 to 64	65 to 74	75 and Over
11.1%	8.6%	7.2%	6.3%	6.5%	4.3%	5.5%
2.1%	2.4%	2.5%	1.9%	2.1%	1.3%	0.9%
5.0%	5.0%	5.0%	4.9%	4.5%	3.1%	1.2%
0.1%	0.2%	0.5%	1.7%	4.0%	8.8%	23.3%
80.4%	82.6%	83.3%	84.3%	81.8%	81.8%	68.3%
7.5%	5.0%	4.8%	4.6%	5.1%	5.8%	5.8%
4.7%	4.9%	3.9%	3.1%	2.0%	1.2%	0.7%
7.1%	7.7%	7.4%	6.9%	5.3%	3.3%	1.5%
0.9%	2.1%	3.5%	8.5%	20.3%	41.9%	69.4%
78.8%	79.6%	79.8%	76.2%	66.7%	47.3%	22.3%

Source: U.S. Bureau of the Census, *Current Population Reports,* Series P-20, No. 287, "Marital Status and Living Arrangements, March, 1975," U.S. Government Printing Office, Washington, D.C., 1975. Table 1.

Table XI
The Men and Women of Sample A, the Younger Sample

Sample		
Men	32% (40)	
Women	68% (85)	
Marital Status		
Never married	90%	
Divorced	10%	
Marital Plans		
Plan to marry	79%	
Do not plan to marry	21%	
Religious Affiliation		
Catholic	45%	
Jewish	25%	
Protestant	11%	
None	17%	
Other	2%	
Ethnicity		
White	70%	
Italian		18%
Irish		11%
Other white		41%
Puerto Rican	18%	
Black	8%	
Other	4%	
Employment		
Clerical, secretarial, managerial or technical	33%	
Teachers or paraprofessionals	19%	
Nursing or health care	11%	
Service or labor sector	7%	
Sales	6%	
Unemployed	24%	
Mean age total sample	22	

Table XII
The Men and Women of Sample B, the Older Sample

	Men	*Women*
Total number in sample	20	20
Mean age	34	29
Age range	23-62	22-38
Education		
Advanced degree	40%	35%
College Degree only	45%	55%
Some college	15%	10%
Religious affiliation		
Catholic	30%	30%
Jewish	30%	35%
Protestant	40%	35%
Marital experiences*		
Married once	40%	35%
Married twice	5%	5%
Had previous exclusive heterosexual relationship	30%	40%
Never married or lived in exclusive heterosexual relationship	35%	35%

*Some of the previously married respondents had also had previous exclusive heterosexual relationships.

Table XII
The Number and Strength of Schism A and Other Strata

EXPERIMENTS AND EXPLORATIONS

- Ask five to ten of your friends what comes to their minds when you say the word *single*. Then try the word *married*. What was the first word association? It's an interesting way to find out how your friends see married and single persons.

- Were you expected to marry? If so, what were your earliest recollections of messages about marriage? Who conveyed the messages and how were they conveyed? Why were you expected to marry? If you were *not* expected to marry, why not? And how were those messages conveyed?

- Pick any five records, books, television shows, movies or plays and try to describe how love is defined in them.

- When and how did you learn about sexual behavior, and to what extent have your ideas changed over the years?

- Is there an area in your town with a high concentration of young adults? Where is this "youth ghetto"? How did it get to be there and what is its history? Who lived there before and who lives there now?

- What does your local zoning ordinance say about unrelated individuals living together? Are there limits to the number of unrelated individuals who can share a place? What kinds of housing are available for singles who live together as a group?

- Which of the pushes and pulls listed in Chapter 6 have you experienced in your life? Which do you experience now?

- Take a friend and visit the nearest bar, club, or resort catering to singles. Note the location, the number of men and women there, their ages, their dress, what they say, how they stand, what they drink, who initiates contact and conversation, who buys the drinks, and what activities are available. Speak to some of the people and ask them why they are there, how often they've been there—and if they are enjoying themselves.

• Pick any ten television commercials or advertisements in a newspaper or magazine and attempt to determine what audience each is addressing. Are any of the ads or commercials aimed at singles? What is the message and what is being sold?

• Is it easier for you to have same-sex or opposite-sex friends? Why?

INTERVIEWING SCHEDULE

1. Age

2. Sex

3. Marital Status

4. Occupation

5. Religion

6. Place of birth

7. What was the last year of school you completed?

8. What was your parents' education?

9. Do you consider yourself:
   a. very conservative
   b. somewhat conservative
   c. disinterested/neutral
   d. somewhat liberal
   e. very liberal
   f. radical

10. What is/are the first word(s) that come into your mind when you hear the word "single"?

11. Why aren't you married?

12. Have you ever been married, and if so, why did you marry?

13. Have you ever lived in a sexually exclusive relationship with someone? Opposite sex? Same sex?

14. If so, what were your experiences in the relationship?

15. If so, how long did each of these relationships last? Why did it break up?

16. What are your current thoughts about marriage? Do you think that you will ever marry? If yes, under what sorts of circumstances? What conditions, if any, would you impose on such an arrangement?

17. Do you think that being single will be a permanent status for you?

18. What pressures and pulls do/did you feel toward getting married?

19. Did/do your parents expect you to marry? If so, how are or were these expectations conveyed? When did they start conveying the expectations?

20. Did relatives pressure you into getting married?

21. As you were growing up, did you and your friends talk about marriage? What was said? Did you talk about weddings? What was said? What sort of person constituted a *"good catch?"* What were your fantasies?

22. What and when was your first recollection of wanting (or not wanting) to get married?

23. *Now,* do you and your friends talk, fantasize, rehearse, etc. about marriage and weddings?

24. Is there one person or an experience that made you decide to stay single at this time? What or who was it?

25. How do you feel society regards single people?

26. Have people ever suggested that you were immature, irresponsible, gay, or something else for not being married? Do

you ever think of yourself as a deviant or different because
you are single?

27. Who do you feel gives you the most support?

28. Do you see a therapist or counselor? If so, do you feel that
they would like to see you married?

29. What is your current dating situation?

30. How many people of the opposite sex do you date?

31. Is there one person you date exclusively or almost exclusively?

32. Do you think that you will marry that person eventually?

33. Where do you meet people of the opposite sex?

34. How satisfying were these places? Would/did you ever go back?

35. How do you feel about one night stands?

36. What is your current living arrangement? How happy are you
with this arrangement?

37. Who do you spend your time with?

38. What is your definition of a friend? How many close male/
female friends do you have? How often do you see them?

39. What are your expectations of a friend?

40. Is it easier for you to have the same- or opposite-sex friends?
Do you have different expectations from same- and opposite-
sex friends? What are they? Who would you be most likely
to seek out with a problem? With good news?

41a. Do you feel that having a sexual relationship supports friendship? Do you make a distinction between friends and those you're sexually involved with? Between friends and lovers? Is or was your best friend also your husband/wife/lover?

41b. Do you feel that you set up boundaries for yourself around friendships?

41c. How easy or difficult is it for you to develop friendships?

42. What does having sex mean to you?

43. Do you ever feel possessive, jealous, and competitive around sex? How so? How do you feel when you think these things? How do you deal with them?

44. Do you feel that you have to be "in love" or care for someone deeply before you have sex?

45. How does sex affect your self-esteem? How important is sex for you?

46. Do you have any limits for yourself around sex? What are these limits?

47. What groups or organizations do you belong to? Women's, men's groups?

48. How and in what way does membership in a men's or women's group affect your life as a single person?

49. Do you feel any pressures from colleagues and/or work associates to marry? If yes, what form does it take?

50. Have you ever felt discriminated against because you are single? Re: hiring, salary, promotion, invitations to work-related activities.

51. Have you ever felt discriminated against regarding the following: bank loans, credit ratings, charge accounts, major purchases (cars), real estate, housing and renting (alone or with group), travel, education—admission to school or financial aid?

52. Have you ever felt any other discrimination because you are single? Because of your sex?

53. Do you feel that a single man or woman of your ethnic group faces unique problems? Why?

54. Do you feel constrained to date within your own ethnic group? Do you date outside your group?

55. It is 1985. Describe your living and marital situation.

56. Is there anything else that you feel you want to tell us about marriage, being single, and so forth? Thank you very much for your time.

BIBLIOGRAPHY

ADAMS, BERT. *Kinship in an Urban Setting.* Chicago: Markham Publishing Co., 1968.

ADAMS, MARGARET. "The Single Woman in Today's Society." In Arlene Skolnick and Jerome Skolnick (eds.), *Intimacy, Family and Society.* Boston: Little, Brown, 1974.

_____. *Single Blessedness.* New York: Basic Books, 1976.

ALLON, NATALIE AND DIANE FISHEL. "The Urban Courting Patterns: Singles' Bars." Paper Presented at the Annual American Sociological Association Meeting, New York, August, 1973.

ANDERSON, CHARLES. *The Political Economy of Social Class.* Englewood Cliffs, N.J.: Prentice-Hall, Inc., 1974.

BABCHUCK, NICHOLAS AND ALAN BOOTH. "Voluntary Association Membership." *American Sociological Review* 34 (1969): 31-45.

BATES, ALAN. "Parental Roles in Courtship." *Social Forces* 20 (1942): 483-486.

BELL, ROBERT. *Marriage and Family Interaction.* 3rd ed. Homewood, Ill.: Dorsey, 1971.

_____.*Marriage and Family Interaction.* 4th ed. Homewood, Ill.: Dorsey, 1975.

BERGER, PETER. *Invitation to Sociology: A Humanistic Perspective.* New York: Doubleday & Co., Inc., Anchor Books, 1963.

BERNARD, JESSIE. *Remarriage.* New York: Dryden Press, 1956.

_____. *The Future of Marriage.* New York: World Publishing Company, 1972.

_____. "Note on Changing Life Styles, 1970-1974." *Journal of Marriage and the Family* 37 (1975): 3.

BERSON, BARBARA, AND BEN BOVA. *Survival Guide for the Suddenly Single.* New York: St. Martin's Press, 1974.

BIRD, CAROLINE. "The Case Against Marriage." In Louise Kapp Howe (ed.), *The Future of the Family.* New York: Simon and Schuster, 1972.

BOOTH, ALAN. "Sex and Social Participation." *American Sociological Review* 37 (1972): 183-192.

BRADFORD, DAVID AND SIMON KLEVANSKY. "Non-Utopian Communities—The Middle Class." In Kenneth Kammeyer (ed.), *Confronting the Issues.* Boston: Allyn and Bacon, 1975.

BRANDWEIN, RUTH, CAROL BROWN, AND ELIZABETH MAURY FOX. "Women and Children Last: The Social Situation of Divorced Mothers and Their Families." *Journal of Marriage and the Family,* 36 (1974): 498-514.

BRIM, ORVILLE G. "Socialization Through the Life Cycle." In Orville Brim and Stanton Wheeler (eds.), *Socialization After Childhood.* New York: Wiley, 1966.

BRODERICK, CARLFRED, AND GEORGE ROWE. "A Scale of Pre-adolescent Heterosexual Development." *Journal of Marriage and the Family.* 30 (1968): 97-101.

BROWN, HELEN GURLEY. *Sex and the Single Girl.* New York: Random House, 1962.

CHOMSKY, NOAM. *Language and Mind.* New York: Harcourt, Brace & World, 1968.

COGSWELL, BETTY AND MARVIN SUSSMAN. "Changing Family and Marriage Forms: Complications for Human Service Systems." *The Family Coordinator* 21 (1972): 505-516.

COOPER, DAVID. *The Death of the Family.* New York: Pantheon Books, 1970.

DANZIGER, CARL AND MATTHEW GREENWALD. *Alternatives: A Look at Unmarried Couples and Communes.* New York: Institute for Life Insurance, 1974.

DOMHOFF, G. WILLIAM. *Who Rules America?* Englewood Cliffs, N.J.: Prentice-Hall, Inc., 1967.

_____. *The Higher Circles.* New York: Random House, 1970.

DOUVAN, ELIZABETH, AND JOSEPH ADELSON. *The Adolescent Experience.* New York: John Wiley & Sons, Inc., 1966.

DUBERMAN, LUCILE. *Marriage and Its Alternatives.* New York: Praeger, 1974.

_____. *The Reconstituted Family.* Chicago: Nelson-Hall, 1975.

DURKHEIM, EMILE. *Suicide: A Study in Sociology,* trans. by John A. Spaulding and G. Simpson. 1897. Reprint. New York: Free Press, 1951.

EDWARDS, MARIE, AND ELEANOR HOOVER. *The Challenge of Being Single.* Los Angeles: J. P. Tarcher, Inc., 1974.

EHRLICH, HOWARD, NATALIE SOKOLOFF, FRED PINCUS, AND CAROL EHRLICH. *Women and Men: A Socioeconomic Factbook.* Baltimore, MD.: Research Group One, 1975.

FLACKS, RICHARD. *Youth and Social Change.* Chicago: Markham Publishing Co., 1971.

GILBERT, EUGENE. "The Youth Market." *The Journal of Marketing.* 36 (1972): 73.

GILDER, GEORGE. *Naked Nomads.* New York: Quadrangle, 1974.

GLICK, PAUL C. "Some Recent Changes in American Families." *Current Population Reports,* P-23, No. 52 (1975).

————. AND ARTHUR J. NORTON. "Perspectives on the Recent Upturn in Divorce and Remarriage." *Demography* 10 (1973): 301-314.

GOODE, WILLIAM. *Women in Divorce.* New York: Free Press, 1956.

GOULD, ROBERT E. "Measuring Masculinity by the Size of a Paycheck." In Joseph H. Pleck and Jack Sawyer (eds.), *Men and Masculinity.* Englewood Cliffs, N.J.: Prentice-Hall, Inc., 1974.

GREENWALD, MATTHEW AND CARL DANZIGER. "Transadulthood: An Emerging Stage of Life." Unpublished Manuscript, 1975.

GURIN, G., J. VEROFF, AND S. FELD. *Americans View Their Mental Health.* New York: Basic Books, Inc., 1972.

HENRY, JULES. *Pathways to Madness.* New York: Random House, 1972.

HILTZ, ROXANNE. *Creating Community Services for Widows.* Port Washington, Long Island: Kennikat Press (forthcoming).

HUNT, MORTON. *Sexual Behavior in the 1970s.* Chicago: Playboy Press, 1974.

INSTITUTE OF LIFE INSURANCE. *Youth 1974.* New York: Institute of Life Insurance, 1974.

————. *Current Social Issues.* New York: Institute of Life Insurance, 1976. (unpublished data).

JACOBY, SUSAN. "49 Million Singles Can't All Be Right." *The New York Times Magazine.* 17 February 1974: 13, 41-49.

KENISTON, KENNETH. *Young Radicals: Notes on Committed Youth.* New York: Harcourt, Brace & World, Inc., 1968.

————. *Youth and Dissent: The Rise of a New Opposition.* New York: Harcourt, Brace, Jovanovich, Harvest Books, 1971.

KILLIAN, LEWIS. *"Social Movements." In Society Today,* 2nd ed. Del Mar, Calif.: CRM Books, 1973.

KINSEY, ALFRED C., WARDELL B. POMEROY, AND CLYDE E. MARTIN. *Sexual Behavior in the Human Male.* Philadelphia: W. B. Saunders Co., 1948.

————. WARDELL B. POMEROY, AND PAUL H. GEBHART. *Sexual Behavior in the Human Female.* Philadelphia: W. B. Saunders Co., 1953.

KNUPFER, GENEVIEVE, ET AL. "The Mental Health of the Unmarried." *The American Journal of Psychiary,* 122 (1966): 841-851.

KOMAROVSKY, MIRRA. "Cultural Contradictions and Sex Roles: The Masculine Case." *The American Journal of Sociology* 79 (1973): 873-884.

KUHN, MANFRED. "How Mates are Sorted." In Howard Becker and Rueben Hill (eds.), *Family, Marriage and Parenthood.* Boston: Heath, 1955.

KUHN, THOMAS. *The Structure of Scientific Revolution.* Chicago: University of Chicago Press, 1962.

LAING, R. D., AND AARON ESTERSON. *Sanity, Madness and the Family.* Baltimore: Penguin Books, 1970.

LEMASTERS, E. E. *Parents in Modern America.* Homewood, Illinois: Dorsey Press, 1974.

LEVIN, ROBERT AND AMY LEVIN. *The Redbook Report: A Study of Female Sexuality.* New York: *Redbook* Magazine, 1975.

LEVINSON, DANIEL. "The Sociology of the Life Cycle: The Middle Years." Remarks of the Presider in a Session at the Annual Convention, American Sociological Association, San Francisco August 1975.

LEVINSON, DANIEL, ET AL. "The Psychosocial Development of Men in Early Adulthood and the Mid-life Transition." In D. F. Ricks, A. Thomas, and M. Roff (eds.), *Life History Research in Psychopathology,* vol. III. Minneapolis: University of Minnesota Press, 1974.

LOPATA, HELENA ZNANIECKI. *Widowhood in an American City.* Cambridge: Schenkman, 1973.

MACKLIN, ELEANOR. "Comparison of Parent and Student Attitudes Toward Non-marital Cohabitation." Paper presented at NCFR Annual Meeting, St. Louis, Missouri, October, 1974.

_____. "Heterosexual Cohabitation Among Unmarried College Students." *Family Coordinator* 21 (1972): 463-472.

MEAD, MARGARET. *Culture and Commitment.* New York: Natural History Press/Doubleday, 1970.

MYERS, ROBERT. "Marketing Opportunities." *Business Horizons* (February 1972): 325-335.

PARENT, GAIL. *Sheila Levine is Dead and Living in New York.* New York: Bantam, 1973.

PLECK, JOSEPH H. "Man to Man: Is Brotherhood Possible?" In Nona Glazer-Malbin (ed.), *Old Family/New Family.* New York: D. Van Nostrand Co., 1975.

_____. AND JACK SAWYER. (EDS.), *Men and Masculinity.* Englewood Cliffs, N.J.: Prentice-Hall, Inc., 1974.

RAMEY, JAMES. *Intimate Friendships.* Englewood Cliffs, N.J.: Prentice-Hall, Inc., 1976.

SELIGSON, MARSHA. *The Eternal Bliss Machine.* New York: Bantam, 1974.

SIMON, WILLIAM AND JOHN H. GAGNON. "Psychosexual Development." In Arlene Skolnick and Jerome Skolnick (eds.), *Intimacy, Family and Society.* Boston: Little, Brown, 1974.

SKOLNICK, ARLENE. *The Intimate Environment.* Boston: Little, Brown, 1973.

SLATER, PHILIP. *The Pursuit of Loneliness.* Boston: Beacon Press, 1970.

SROLE, LEO, ET AL. *Mental Health in the Metropolis: The Midtown Manhattan Study.* New York: McGraw-Hill Co., 1962.

_____. "Midtown Manhattan Mental Health Restudy" (forthcoming).

STAPLES, ROBERT. *The World of Black Singles* (In Preparation).

STARR, JOYCE, AND DONALD CARNS. "Singles in the City." *Society* 9 (1972): 43-48.

STEIN, PETER. "The Impact of the Family, Education and the Social-historical Context on the Values of College Students." Unpublished Ph.D. dissertation, Princeton University, 1969.

_____. "Changing Attitudes of College Women." Unpublished manuscript, Rutgers University, 1973.

TURNER, RALPH. *Family Interaction.* New York: John Wiley & Sons, Inc., 1970.

UDRY, J. RICHARD. *The Social Context of Marriage.* Philadelphia: J. B. Lippincott Co., 1974.

U.S. BUREAU OF THE CENSUS. *Current Population Reports,* P-20, no. 271, "Marital Status and Living Arrangements: March 1974." Washington, D.C.: 1974.

_____ *Current Population Reports,* P-20, no. 287, "Marital Status and Living Arrangements: March 1975." Washington, D.C.: 1975.

WALLER, WILLARD. "The Rating and Dating Complex." *American Sociological Review* 2 (1937): 727-737.

WEKERLE, GERDA. "Vertical Village: Social Contacts in a Single Highrise Complex." Faculty of Environmental Studies, York University. Toronto, Canada, 1975.

YANKELOVICH, DANIEL. *The Changing Values on Campus.* New York: Washington Square Press, 1972.

YATES, MARTHA. *Coping: A Survival Manual for Women Alone.* Englewood Cliffs, N.J.: Prentice-Hall, Inc., 1975.

ZABLOCKI, BENJAMIN. *Urban Communes Project.* Columbia University 1975, unpublished data.

Index